TOMORROW'S AMERICAN

THE WEIL LECTURES OF 1976

Tomorrow's

American

EDITED BY

Samuel

Sandmel

NEW YORK

OXFORD UNIVERSITY PRESS

1977

COPYRIGHT © 1977 BY OXFORD UNIVERSITY PRESS, INC.

LIBRARY OF CONGRESS CATALOGUE CARD NUMBER: 76-42648

PRINTED IN THE UNITED STATES OF AMERICA

INTRODUCTION

The lectures given under the auspices of the Frank L. Weil Institute for Studies in Religion and the Humanities have usually been a series of six given by one scholar. The Weil Lectures for 1976, coming at a time of the American Bicentennial and the Centennial of the Hebrew Union College–Jewish Institute of Religion, where the Weil Institute is located, have been, instead, a series of eight lectures, each by a different person. They were given in January and February.

It was the intent of the Institute that each of the eight lecturers deal with a major significant aspect of American life, and they were asked to prepare their manuscripts with a general audience in view. It was hoped that each lecture would begin with a factual basis and proceed to draw the relevant moral or ethical implications. It was not expected that the lecturers would predict the future, but rather that they would project what the future portends and, in that context, point to the moral dilemmas or moral decisions that lie ahead.

The lectures are arranged in the order in which they were given. Sadly, it must be recorded here that Mr. Alistair Buchan died in England a month after he had given his lecture, the first in the series. He was the only lecturer who was not an American, yet one sensed from association with him during the period of his visit how deep was his concern for this, his host country. Expressions of that concern are to be found in his lecture.

Samuel Sandmel, CHAIRMAN
EXECUTIVE COMMITTEE

CINCINNATI, OHIO

CONTENTS

TOMORROW'S AMERICAN

I

ALASTAIR
BUCHAN

THE UNITED
STATES

Let me begin by expressing the sense of pride and honor that I feel that this distinguished Institute should have invited a foreigner from what is now a weak and deeply troubled sister nation to give the first of this important series of lectures. It happens that I was brought up by a man, unusual among the British of his generation, who had a considerable knowledge and profound affection for the United States: and that I have been commuting back and forth across the cold, gray ocean that divides our two countries for just over forty years. Nevertheless, your invitation is symbolic of the openness and social generosity that has been a central characteristic of American society in the past half century.

If one accepted the full logic of what is now called "linkage politics," an ugly phrase for a classic conception for which writers such as

IN TOMORROW'S INTERNATIONAL SYSTEM

Montesquieu and Burke had a simpler language, namely that a country's foreign policy is largely an extrapolation of the domestic needs and stresses of its own society, then clearly this lecture should have been the last in the series, not the first. The fact that it is the first is due to the kindness of the Institute, for my academic obligations would have made it impossible for me to come later. But it may also be right that it should be the first, for the day is past when this country, despite its economic power, despite its continental size, can debate its own economic and social and institutional problems without reference to the external world on which they react and which reacts on them.

Let me start with two points of definition. First, what do we mean by the international system? Clearly it is not simply a calculus of the relative power of states and of their interaction upon each other; it is not simply a matter of diplomatic or interstate relationships, especially in the days of great multinational corporations and of mass communication; this is only one aspect of it. It is also a matter of the internal strength or weaknesses of different societies. And by reason of this it is also a matter of what states and societies conceive to be their high priorities, their vital interests if you like, what people care about. It has thus a structural and qualitative aspect, who can do what, and what is on the agenda of high politics in any epoch.

Second, what does one mean by "tomorrow"? I believe that social science, like meteorology, has become bedeviled by an attempt to reach beyond its grasp; to assert a predictive capacity to which it has no valid claim. Of course one can study long-term trends and see whether they are gathering or losing force. Of course one can set up models of different futures, and indeed, as Daniel Bell has often pointed out, this is an important aid to moral choice. Of course, the statesman with some insight into the future looms larger in the history books than he misjudges it.[1] Of course governments who must order weapons systems or power stations that will not be produced or perfected for ten or fifteen years have to make assumptions about the future, even though in the course of making them they also influence that future. But the more high flown attempts at long-range futurology of the past decade have, for the most part, been laughed out of court. Dr. Herman Kahn's book on *The Year 2000*, for instance, written, I think, in 1970, hardly mentions the word "oil."

I cannot tell you what the international system of A.D. 2000 will resemble, what the attitudes and preoccupations of a generation that is still unborn will be or what the American priorities will be. Although I think it likely that America will still be the most powerful state, I propose to set my sights at a more modest elevation and discuss the visible horizon, say the fifteen years that will elapse between the time an able young American enters a good law school now and the time he takes his seat in Congress.

The international system in which we dwell today, dominated as

---

[1] This might be said to be the difference between Bismarck and de Gaulle. "People who look forward and grasp the essential facts which will govern the future groupings of nations may be able to assert profound influence on the political future of the world" (A. J. Balfour, 1909).

far as issues of security are concerned by two superpowers coexisting by reason of a complex system of strategic deterrence, a non-communist world that contains a group of very highly developed states, plus a graduation of prospering, poor, and very poor countries: and twice the number of legally sovereign states that existed twenty years ago, is very much of America's own devising. The whole nuclear relationship is a consequence of the American genius for technological organization, for I personally doubt whether a country that, in the late 1940's, was attempting to recover from the most cruel war in its history, namely, the Soviet Union, would, even under Stalin, have put many resources into a nuclear weapons program if the United States had not demonstrated in 1945 that it could be accomplished. The division of Europe into an east-west confrontation was likely, but it was made inevitable not only by mutual Anglo-American and Soviet misperceptions of each other's needs and fears, but by our overestimate of Soviet capabilities. The regeneration of Europe and Japan was partly the consequence of highly intelligent acts of American politico-economic statesmanship. The rapid calling into existence of a large number of new weak states was also partly, though not entirely, a consequence of American historical attitudes toward colonialism. More important, it was also the consequence of a hubristic belief that sprang from the confidence of an earlier generation of Americans in their own society, that the United States could successfully enter into a relationship with areas and societies of which she then knew little, in Southern or Southeast Asia, or the Islamic world.

I am not emphasizing this fact to point any finger of accusation at the United States. In any case, as one of our own great historians, Lewis Namier, used to warn his students, it is no good "arguing with history," trying to abstract one or more variables from the past to pass any moral judgment on how history might have been written differently. The very sense of the universality of American interests over the whole globe that contributed to the Cold War in Europe and led to the Vietnam debacle in Asia led also to a multilateral trade and payments system which has produced the greatest rise in well-being and prosperity in human history, and which has stood up remarkably well so far in a period of serious recession.

I make the point for a different reason: namely, I find many serious Americans who are now depressed and disturbed that the United

States has brought into being an international order which she cannot effectively mediate, moderate, lead, and, in the last instance, control. I think this is a real problem that will be with us through the "tomorrow" at which we are looking. If it is ignored, it might lead to an illusion about America's ability to insulate itself from an ungrateful world. If it is gotten out of focus it can lead to a kind of chauvinism that may assuage popular emotions but will not advance the interests either of the United States or of world order.

In 1967 a very acute American political scientist, George Liska, wrote a book in which he suggested that the United States had the characteristics of one of the great historic empires of antiquity, not the recent mercantile empires like the British or the Dutch, "because of its great margin for error."[2] It is curious how, as Hegel said, "the owl of Minerva flies only in the evening," for those words were written at the precise moment when this was ceasing to be true: a year before the decision that the Vietnam war was a hopeless cause, just as the Soviet Union was beginning to draw equal to the United States in strategic power, and just three years before the collapse of the dollar as the basic western currency. Despite the fact that the United States largely brought the present international system into being, it has not only lost its margin for error, but it has now much more the character of a large state than the center of the universe—at least the non-communist universe—which it had for perhaps the twenty-five years after 1941. There is, however, one special qualification to this statement to which I will later return.

Because of this change, because we have emerged into a more multilateral world order—an order in which the Shah of Iran can snap his fingers at us, in which Mrs. Gandhi can foreclose the whole system of democratic government which was the basis of the western relationship with India and we can do nothing about it—because the European Community is beginning to acquire somewhat different, though not irreconcilable, interests from the United States; because there is a whole new order of business with the developing world, it is as well to avoid broad generalizations and to look specifically at the most important American relationships with the external world.

And the right place to start is obviously with the central power

[2] *Imperial America: The International Politics of Primacy*, John Hopkins Press, p. 29.

relationship between the United States and the Soviet Union. It is a striking fact that of the 105 treaties and agreements that have been signed since the United States and the Soviet Union entered diplomatic relations in 1933, 58 were concluded between 1969 and the spring of 1975. It is a comforting fact that there is a degree of consultation and mutual comprehension between Washington and Moscow that significantly diminishes the risk of, say, another Cuban missile crisis. It is a civilizing factor that there is now a marked degree of cooperation on medical, environmental, and other forms of research. It is a remarkable fact that a Soviet spacecraft and an American one can successfully unite in outer space. But such isolated developments do not necessarily provide a solid foundation for continuing détente.

In the first place, the strategic balance has now reached a point of complexity where it is not clear whether further negotiations can do more than set margins to the arms race, rather than markedly reduce the level of the balance to one which a rising generation, one not reared in the atmosphere of the Cold War, can find intelligible and so be ready to sustain. Technological innovations that in the late 1950's and early 1960's worked in favor of a stable superpower relationship—say, hardened missiles or Polaris submarines—now also work against it, thus multiple warheads and improved accuracies engender mutual fears of a disarming attack. Second, since what has been achieved is simply détente and since both superpowers have different aspirations that, in Secretary Kissinger's words, "do not spring from misunderstanding, or personalities, or transitory factors,"[3] but are rooted in history and nourished by conflicting values, their competition for influence within the international system is only muted, not resolved. Third, such détente as has been attained has come about through a process of purely political negotiatons, and has almost no social and only a modest economic content, unlike, say, the *entente cordiale* of the European-American relationship in NATO. It has been a consequence of intergovernmental agreement and as such could be reversed by successor regimes. It is based, moreover, on mutual strategic deterrence with weapons of enormous destructive power, and this, though it may inhibit war between the great powers, is inherently a relationship of antagonism that would make social rapprochement difficult even if the suspicious element in the Russian

3 Statement made before the Senate foreign relations committee, Sept. 19, 1974.

national character would tolerate it. Finally, because both powers are enormous and heterogeneous societies, intergovernmental agreements are vulnerable to the interplay of each other's domestic politics. The Soviet cancellation in January 1975 of the 1972 Soviet-American trade agreement by reason of the terms that Congress set upon it and the paucity of American credits by comparison with Soviet expectations, or Soviet interventions in the American grain market, are cases in point.

The maintenance of superpower détente will not be easy over the next decade, which is not to say it is impossible. One difficulty arises from uncertainty about the nature of the American political temper, about what will be the balance between and within the parties and where the balance between Congressional and Executive power will come to rest, for political introversion could give rise to a passive conception of détente, one that simply accepts the achievements of the past and has no dynamism. Another is ignorance about the impending change in the leadership of the Soviet Union and what it means—whether it will pass to a man like Kinslenko, whether it will pass to some younger and more adventurous figure, or what the influence of the military will be. Second, the disarray of western economic and energy relationships creates a host of uncertainties, including the possibility that a more dynamic Soviet leadership than today's might see in it that "crisis of capitalism" which would impel a challenge to the principle of coexistence, if not at the center, then on the peripheries of the western system. Third, there is the question of whether human judgment can control the dynamism of technological change, as the difficulties with the second round of this SALT negotiations have illustrated. Mutual uncertainty about the nature of the central strategic balance is more probable than a simple transference of strategic superiority from the United States to the Soviet Union. Finally, there is the danger that the western industrialized powers may become involved in a confrontation with the more militant developing countries, a conflict in which not only might the Soviet Union be *tertius gaudens* but which might strike the spark of military conflict, especially in the Mediterranean.

When the "containment" policy was fashioned in the late 1940's, it was conceived as being necessary only for a limited time span, until, that is, the Soviet Union recognized the limitations of revolutionary or nationalist policies and turned to other preoccupations; until other centers of power than the United States regained their strength and the international system reverted to its normal plural state. Some of the objectives of the containment policy have been attained. Insofar as ideological hostility has been a source of conflict between the Soviet Union and the capitalist world, it has been partly overlaid by practical considerations of security or welfare politics. This is not true of the rivalry between the two great communist powers. As a result, the United States no longer shoulders the burden alone; and, ironically, in the area where the containment policy was criticized as being inapplicable, namely in the Far East and Asia, much of the political task of containing Soviet power is exercised not only by the United States but also by China, so that the former is, or need only be, one party in a multiple balance. But the Soviet Union has also become a very powerful military state of a traditional kind with a global reach, like France in the eighteenth century or Britain in the nineteenth.

This leads one naturally to a consideration of the American relationship to the Sino-Soviet conflict where there is deep and perhaps growing hostility. It is not difficult to see why this is so. In the first place, Mao and Stalin made quite contrary deductions in terms of policy from the writings of Marx, differences arising out of a wholly different cultural and historical approach to a corpus of Teutonic theory. Those of you who know the history of relations between the two communist parties will recall that this mutual contempt for each others' views winds back for nearly fifty years. Second, there is an inherent disposition to racism in the temperament of Greater Russians which can be eliminated if they live in a liberal state like this, to which many of them emigrated, but is fed by a sense of national xenophobia for those that remain. Thus they delude themselves with imaginary scenarios of 800 million Chinese sweeping across Asia to engulf them under some modern Genghis Khan. This disposition to racism is also having serious effects within the Soviet Union as the southern republics grow in population, and it is one of the reasons why the Russians are unlikely to have a successful or enduring influence in Angola. Third, the two powers share the longest frontier in the world, nearly twice the length of the Canadian-American border, and it is very easy for tension to develop on land borders that are not marked by mountain ranges or natural features. Finally, there is a profound sense of rancor in China where the Soviet Union is concerned, growing out of a sense both of historical injustice and present-day fear.

It is idle to speculate how the Sino-Soviet relationship may develop, since we stand, as it were, near the deathbeds of the absolute leaders of both countries. But in my view the evolution of even a cold peace may take longer than "tomorrow," unless we in the west are stupid enough to frighten both states into some new and artificial entente. At the same time it is not a western interest to exacerbate it, as some people thought it might be ten years ago. To do so would create appalling problems for Japan, which depends on trade with both. Worse still, it would heighten that same Soviet xenophobia that is so easily aroused, and induce that same sense of being trapped between an adversary on either flank that Franco-Russian diplomacy induced in Germany in the twenty years before World War I. In fact, an amelioration of Sino-Soviet relations is, I think in our interest, for it would make for a less competitive attitude to problems like terrorism in the Philippines or the MPLA in Angola, and for the reason I have given I still see little prospect of resuscitating that famous Sino-Soviet bloc whose existence so mesmerized Washington in the early 1960's, after its reality had begun to disappear.

But, this said, how much influence the United States can exert upon the amelioration of Sino-Soviet relations is very hard to guess. Secretary Kissinger has done his best to prevent them from getting worse, and the European leaders, Helmut Schmidt, Giscard d'Estaing, and Edward Heath, who have visited Peking and whose governments are persistently badgered by the Chinese to adopt a more militant attitude toward Russia, have politely declined to do so. What I am certain is important is to avoid getting involved in guileful Chinese diplomatic maneuvers or attempts to manipulate the balance of power in her favor.

This brings me back to the question of détente. We know that there is no question of dominance as far as American relations with either the Soviet Union or China are concerned. Secretary Kissinger has brought into being a trilateral balance of power, and this has written off some of the dangers and distortions of the past: indeed, it seemed at first that because China and Russia are bitter enemies at present the United States might find itself with the greatest leverage of the three. But we know both in terms of historical experience and current reality that a tripolar balance in the sense of an equilateral triangle cannot be indefinitely sustained: it leads to distrust at each corner of the triangle; it creates the temptation to sustain equilibrium at the expense of third parties, as happened in Europe in the eighteenth century and could happen now again in relation to parts of the developing world. It tends to drag the United States into what are essentially Sino-Soviet contests for influence in the Third World, such as Angola.

Since we cannot at present have a five-power balance, which is the basic model of stability, because Japan and western Europe are not political actors of equivalent weight to the other three, the United States has to make a choice as to whether it is Peking or Moscow with whom it has the more constructive agenda of negotiation. And in my view there is no question that it is with the Soviet Union by reason of the potential dangers to the strategic nuclear balance to which I have already referred and by reason of the Soviet influence upon the secondary area of conflict, the Middle East. If there is no SALT agreement this year, then I think the President who leads the United States into its third century will have a very difficult task in establishing strategic stability, let alone in moving on to the reduction of strategic forces which the growing demands from other sources on federal expenditure clearly make of central political interest in this country.

I will not say much about the Japanese-American alliance, because I do not think it will greatly change. If one thinks back to the adversary relationship of the first half of the century, or to the broken, desolate islands of a quarter-century ago, and thinks forward to the dramatic surge of Japanese consumer exports in the later 1960's, the fact that it has held together so well is a real triumph of statecraft for both Tokyo and Washington. One point may be worth making; I think the Japanese have thought very hard in secret about the problems of acquiring nuclear weapons and all the implications of doing so. I think for "tomorrow" they have rejected the idea; whether they have rejected it for good depends partly on what American policy and attitudes are likely to be in fifteen or twenty years' time, and partly on whether the two great mainland powers can move toward a cold peace and some basis of mutual tolerance. I can imagine Japan becoming seriously alarmed either if there were a precipitate withdrawal of American concern with the maintenance of a stable balance in Asia, or if Sino-Soviet hostility were to flare into open conflict, reminding the Japanese people of the inherent vulnerability that geography imposes on them.

I would be remiss if, as a European, I did not go into some detail on the future of European-American relations as well as both European and American interests in the Middle East. We—both Europeans and Americans, that is—have come through a period of considerable disenchantment with illusions that, candidly, we created for ourselves. Because of the need to find a political and social western anchor for a renascent Germany in a Europe which had become split into two hostile systems in the early years of the Cold War, there was not only considerable European but also considerable American enthusiasm for the foundation of the European Economic Community in 1958—American enthusiasm, despite the fact that such a Community was likely also to become a powerful trading rival of the United States.

Then, throughout the Kennedy and Johnson presidencies, we had perforce to live with the phenomenon of de Gaulle, whom perhaps we admire more in retrospect than we did when he was in office. De Gaulle's prime objective was to restore the morale and prestige of France, and to prove that the international system was not wholly dominated by the superpowers.

Unfortunately, in the process of doing so he seriously arrested the development of the community and its institutions. His departure revived hopes on both sides of the Atlantic that it would march forward again, not merely as a coherent economic entity but also as a political one that would relieve America's burdens. The history of the community over the past five or six years has been a very complex one, made more difficult by its enlargement from six to nine to include one major industrial and two small, primarily agricultural states. More than that, it began to try and develop more active Central European institutions of decision-making just at a time when more and more functional areas of activity—monetary relationships for one thing, energy problems for another—were becoming global in character and impossible to handle on a European scale.

The consequence has been that the community has had to lower its sights. It has become clear that not only military security in Europe must continue to be handled on the basis of a multilateral alliance system, NATO, of which the United States, with its vast strategic strength and its continuing interest in the integrity of western Europe, is the leader and the core power. Energy and monetary relations have also to be handled on an Atlantic or global basis. The notion of a bilateral European-American partnership, which seemed so promising fifteen years ago, at present only operates in the more limited field of trade negotiations.

However, it would be a mistake to think that the community is a failure or in a process of decay, even if the more ambitious objective of acquiring the characteristics of a powerful single actor in world politics by the end of this decade is now seen as likely to take much longer to achieve.

For if ideas of creating a super-state with a population larger than that of the United States or the Soviet Union, and nearly equal in economic power to the United States, have proved unrealistic, the community is acquiring quite rapidly the characteristics of an effective political entente. There are several fields of recent political activity in which I think this can be demonstrated. One was the unified position taken by the nine in the Conference on European Security and Cooperation (CESC) at Helsinki and Geneva, which lasted from the beginning of 1973 to the middle of 1975. This was not a diplomatic negotiation that had the highest priority for the United States, which, very understandably, attached prime importance to its bilateral negotiations with the Soviet Union on Stragetic Arms Limitation; it was the nine who forced the Soviet Union to make CESC a serious negotiator on freedom of information and movement in Europe (unfortunately, with rather disappointing results), before agreeing to declarations on the sovereign equality of European states, East Germany in particular, and on respect for territorial boundaries, which was the Soviet motive for convening it in the first place.

A second area with which the community can deal more effectively than the United States is trade relations with those part of the developing world with which its member states have had long experience and whose economic interests are complementary to their own. Hence the various trade agreements with Israel, India, North Africa, and the large group of equatorial African states whose economic ties with the community were codified in the Rome convention of last year (1975).

There is another area of complementary interests and activities that is of greater political significance. Two of the facts that one cannot evade are the decline of American political influence and the symptoms of political decay in southern Europe. They spring from different causes in different countries: in Portugal as a consequence of the chaos resulting from the removal of an old man's hand on the tiller; in Spain from much the same causes in the case of Franco; in Italy from the increasing political strength of the communist party, though its relationship with Moscow is by no means a purely subservient one; in Greece from the United States' fatal compliance with the régime of the military junta; in Turkey from the refusal of the United States Congress to continue to supply military aid after the Turkish invasion of Cyprus in 1974.

Now this may be temporary and in any case there appears to be little Soviet disposition to exploit the decline in American influence, either because Brezhnev is an old man or because he and his colleagues are preoccupied with China and with the gross failure of their own agricultural system. We have, moreover, learned a lot since the early years of this century, and it is no longer necessarily true that "if the Balkans sneeze, Europe catches cold."

But southern Europe and the Mediterranean have acquired a different significance for the United States from the period beginning nearly thirty years ago when she first established a Mediterranean fleet to contain Soviet influence there. By this I mean that it has become a vital supply line and channel of communication with Israel, to whose survival and integrity as a nation most civilized countries are committed but which commits the United States more deeply than any other for reasons that we need not argue.

Now it happens that as American influence in southern Europe has declined, the influence of the community has not. The Italian communist leaders have made it very clear that they wish any government they may join to remain in it. Greece has applied for full membership, and Turkey has associate status. Moreover, in the eastern Mediterranean there is a useful complementarity of diplomatic influence among its leading members: Britain has direct responsibilities in Cyprus; France has long affinities with Greece, just as Germany has traditional ties with Turkey. The prospects of their containing conflict in that area if their crisis management is coordinated are, therefore, better than those of the United States, even though they have much smaller military and naval forces in the Mediterranean. Power, certainly military power, "no longer translates automatically into influence," as Henry Kissinger pointed out even before he joined the Nixon administration.

On the other hand, in the very highly armed confrontation that has been allowed to develop between Israel and her neighbors, only the United States now possesses the brute strength for influence. I believe myself that there will be no stabilization of the Arab-Israel conflict until Israel has withdrawn to her 1967 borders, which is a very difficult proposition for a power as small as Israel to confront. I think it will require a mixture of both traditional and novel techniques. On the one hand, the next Secretary of State may have to ask Congress to agree to a formal military alliance with, or guarantee to, Israel—a difficult proposition to put forward since it will have been over twenty years since the country last signed a treaty of alliance and much scorn has been poured on Dulles's pactomania in the interval. On the other, it will require the use of United Nations forces and good offices for any demarcation or division of adversaries to be worked out in Sinai and on the Golan Heights which satisfies the legitimate fears of both Israel and her neighbors. It is because the nine have a complementary role to play, as members of the United Nations and as allies of the United States, that I think it important that we Europeans exercise an effective influence in southern Europe.

I would like to conclude with two more general points about the United States and its relations to the international system. The first concerns the developing world. When the United States first entered world politics as its most influential member, that is, in the war years, it was inspired by a sense of the universality of its interests: this was clearly expressed in the message Roosevelt sent to Stalin in October 1944, when he feared that Churchill might negotiate some sphere of influence agreement with him on Europe.

"You, naturally, understand," he cabled, "that in this global war there is literally no question, political or military, in which the United States is not interested."

This general stance took juridical form in the United Nations

Charter, of which the United States was the principal architect, as
well as in more specific measures, such as the General Agreement on
Trade and Tariffs. And when the antithetical character of the two
principal political societies, the United States and the Soviet Union,
made the United Nations an instrument of limited usefulness, American energy and initiative was directed toward the creation of regional
collective security and defense alliances—in Europe, around the Pa-
cific littoral, in Southeast Asia, and in the Middle East. Over the years
these have proved to be of varying utility and significance, NATO remaining central at one end of the scale, SEATO largely peripheral to
American interests in the 1970's at the other.

In the meantime, other forms of regionalism have come into being without the inspiration of either superpower—the EEC, the Organization for African Unity, OPEC, the Association of Southeast
Asian Nations, various regional groupings beneath the general um-
brella of OAS. The British Commonwealth, which now comprises
over thirty countries, still has an important functional utility in relations between its less developed and highly developed members, as
does France's association with the once French states of Africa. There
is, therefore, a choice to be made in American policy. Is the United
States still a power of universal interests? I think today's answer is not
very different from yesterday's, though Vietnam made it clear that
there are severe limits in her capabilities. But the techniques may be
different. Is it more profitable to pursue and preserve these interests
by having state-to-state relations with every one of the 130 countries
in the world? Or by dealing with these new groupings when they are
effective, thus placing greater responsibilities on their shoulders? Just
as political tension in southern Europe can probably be handled
more effectively by the community, is not the Organization for African Unity likely to be able to mediate more effectively in Angola, and
to inhibit Soviet adventurism there, than any western intervention?
Will not the oil producing countries mature to the responsibilities
that their new-found wealth requires if we accept the reality of their
strength and try to elicit their cooperation as new members of the
club of the rich rather than threatening them with confrontation? An
international system of so many states, even if the sovereignty of some
of them is only nominal, is very difficult to be a part of, especially for
the strongest and richest state of all. Will it become more manage-

able, for all concerned, if geographical and functional regional cooperation is encouraged? Or might this simply lead to new forms of
confrontation? I am inclined to the former view, which was, indeed,
the essence of the Nixon doctrine of six years ago. But the question
is not a simple one to answer, though it will increasingly confront
American policy-makers. Do you want coalition with partners of
varying strength? Or is dominance the only stance suitable to your
strength and responsibilities?

I said at an earlier point that the United States today and tomorrow has more the characteristics and the interests of an ordinary great
power than of the dynamic center of the universe, "the last best hope
of man," which she had been for so many people in so many lands
for so many years. John Kennedy's conception of the United States
as the defender of freedom anywhere was drowned in the swamps and
jungles of Vietnam. Watergate was in a sense a blow more crippling
than Vietnam, for it was clearly a consequence not of mistakes, but of
dishonesty in high places. And on top of that have come the C.I.A.
investigations, which may have revealed little that those of us who
happen to know our Washington were not aware of, but are a severe
blow to plain people, here and abroad, who stand amazed that the
world's most powerful democracy had for so long a system of covert
intelligence that was at the same time so pervasive and so inept. The
consequence, I find, is a mood of despondency and often acrimony
here which far outstrips the justification for it. As a Canadian friend
of mine has written, "What worries us most is a loss of faith by Americans in America. The United States is so powerful—militarily, economically, morally—that it can be disciplined only by its own
people."[4]

I not only agree with this but go further and suggest that the
power and influence of the United States in the world is as much dependent on what it is as on what it does; a point that is more readily
appreciated in cities other than New York and Washington. The
United States is still today what it was in the days of Franklin Roosevelt, whom I had the privilege of knowing—namely, the great experimental society of mankind. If it had not been for F.D.R. and the
New Deal, which was not really a governmental program so much as

4 John Holmes, "A View from Another Country," *The Foreign Affairs Kaleido-
scope* (Council on Religion and International Affairs, New York, 1974).

a process of national regeneration, my generation of Europeans would have turned to Marxism as the only answer. If it had not been for Truman's firmness, though it sometimes deteriorated into fierceness, there would have been no western world as we now know it. If it had not been for Eisenhower's patience, which at the time we sometimes thought of as inertia, there would have been no basis on which Kennedy could begin to build bridges to the Soviet Union.

But even more important the way in which the race problem began to be tackled after 1954 showed other societies with racial problems, my own included, how it might be tackled. The way in which serious young American men and women began to address the problem of poverty in the early 1960's had a profound influence on their counterparts in Europe. I can remember when anti-Semitism was a serious social problem in this country; the fact that it has now diminished to trivial proportions here and in other developed countries makes for a more united front in contesting the odious new dictum that Zionism is a form of racism. The fact that the law held over Watergate and did not buckle not only makes figures like Elliot Richardson and Judge Sirica, one a Boston WASP, the other of recent immigrant stock, into rather heroic figures in other countries; it also greatly restored the prestige of the United States abroad.

We who live in smaller countries now governed in the social democratic rather than the liberal tradition think that we have made better progress than you in re-fashioning our great cities or preserving the quality of life. But such developments as the master plan for Detroit are widely studied abroad, and, if you can learn from us, so too we are very ready to learn from you. Similarly, if the power of central government is causing alienation from its authority and creating a need to think through the whole problem of relations between local and central government, I can assure you that we are faced with not identical, but very similar problems.

Finally, there is the important question of the role that the United States will play in the reform and extension of international institutions. In dealing with the state system of the twentieth century the Anglo-American tradition has not been to rely on traditional state-to-state relations alone, but where possible to depend upon international management of problems that can be identified as common to mankind as a whole. Thus both in the Covenant of the

League and in the Charter of the United Nations we tried to subject the problems of war and aggression to a process of international management; that proved unrealistic partly because of conflicts between the great powers, partly because warfare began to acquire completely new dimensions. So to a degree we had to return to the traditional method of restraining conflict, namely balancing military power—with all its difficulties and risks.

But the United Nations remains an important forum for managing the crises that lead to war, as we have seen in many instances over the last decade. And in addition, its specialist agencies have become increasingly important centers for the management and reconciliation of various forms of national activity which impinge on other nations—these are the International Atomic Energy Agency, GATT, the World Health Organization, the new Environmental Protection Organization, and others. These agencies have become more difficult to operate in, especially for a big power with diverse internal pressure groups like the United States, by reason of the rapid growth in the number of sovereign states. They require men of great patience and considerable authority as national representatives: their deliberations are often polemic and their decision-making processes slow. I hope that we may eventually see them reformed by a greater use of the regional principle to which I have referred.

In the meantime, I think it would be a tragedy if the United States with its strong innovative traditions in the field of international law were to lose interest in such international organizations, for they represent one of our best defenses against a return to the international anarchy which Thomas Hobbes described so graphically at the end of the seventeenth century. Instead, I hope that in tomorrow's world, with a federal administration that has a new popular mandate, the immense talents of this country for legal and political improvisation can be applied to many new issues of international management that now confront us: the law of the sea, the activities of multinational companies, the rationalization of raw material prices, energy, the distribution of food supplies, as well as the central political machinery of the United Nations itself.

I have no disposition to minimize the scope and daunting character of the problems that confront this country in a world with a more heterogeneous distribution of power and with a different agenda of high politics than that to which we became accustomed in the post-war era. The old problems, the destabilizing effects of technological innovation upon the central balance of power, the difficulty of controlling domestic unemployment without resorting to the kind of nationalist protectionism that produced the political climate of the 1930's, are, to take only two examples, by no means solved. Problems such as raw material scarcities and high prices, a likely deficiency in world food supplies, terrorism, and increasing trans-national penetration simply lengthen the agenda of international controversy.

There is no prospect of world government in the sense of a universal political federation. But the new problems of an increasingly crowded and fragile world will require a sensitive concern for the common interest, as well as the international regulation of many areas of human activity which have been for centuries in national, or even in private, hands. Otherwise the agenda of high politics, the issues on which states will insist on defending their own interests without reference to the general interest, will become hopelessly overloaded, wires will get crossed, and conflict, major conflict, may occur.

I have often been critical of particular American policies and decisions. I think the coming generation of Americans may have to think very hard about the whole machinery of executive government and its relation not only to Congress but to the people. In a world in which the United States has lost its margin for error, there will clearly have to be a much more careful definition of American interests. But nothing has happened to diminish my own confidence in the creative ability of Americans to meet new challenges and differing responsibilities.

II

DANIEL
BELL

THE

"INTELLIGENTSIA"

IN

The term *intellectual* is used as a noun, more, it is used as a collective noun to designate a group of persons who—the definitions of what they do, or are supposed to do, are so contradictory that one runs into difficulties at the very start in trying to circumscribe, let alone define, their activities—but let us say a group who call *themselves* intellectuals. It may surprise you to learn that the word is of twentieth-century origin. We are so accustomed to using it that we think it has always been there. One reason is that a word, once minted and found useful, quickly becomes read back into time. For example, in Elias Bickerman's *The Historical Foundations of Postbiblical Judaism,* we find:

. . . *The most important result of the Greek impact on Palestinian Judaism was the formation of a Jewish intelligentsia different from*

AMERICAN

SOCIETY

the clergy and not dependent on the sanctuary. The new class was known as "scribes."

The scribe is the secular interpreter of the law; he advises rulers, expounds righteousness. He is not a priest, but an administrator, not concerned with ritual, but with interpretation. "Daniel, who explains the secret and meaning of royal dreams at the Babylonian court, is the ideal scribe as visualized by Ben Sira."

Thus the intellectual is the scribe, the one who discerns the signs of the time, and advises the ruler.

If I turn to an iconoclastic book on Spinoza by Lewis Feuer, he sees the excommunication of that philosopher as a situation where "the theological formulae conceal[ed] the first glimmerings in modern history of the revolutionary Jewish intellectual."

Spinoza is the early prototype of the European Jewish radical. He was a pioneer in forging methods of scientific study in history and politics. He was a cosmopolitan, with scorn for the notion of a privileged people. . . . The Amsterdam Jewish leaders reacted with fear and bewilderment to their first radical intellectual and cast him out from their midst.

Thus the intellectual is the heretic.

I am not concerned with the accuracy of these descriptions, but with the ease with which *intellectual*—in its contradictory way—is used to describe classes and individuals several thousand or several hundred years ago.

Yet if I turn to the *Oxford English Dictionary* (1931) there is a definition of *intellect*—to signify discerning or understanding, though the word was little used in French or English before the sixteenth century. And an intellectual is a person possessing superior powers of intellect. But there is *no* definition in the "ordinary" sense of what we would today call an intellectual.

If you were to look in the *Encyclopaedia Britannica,* even now, you would find *no* article on the intellectual. Nor has there ever been one. Apparently the *Britannica* does not recognize the phenomenon.

Webster's Second (1934) gives three definitions of *intellectual* as an adjective, and three as a noun; the last of these being:

An intellectual person: pl. *such persons as a social class; also* [often cap.] *a member of a party or faction claiming to represent, or regarded as representing intelligent opinion, as the Russian* intellectuals.

And there is a definition of *intelligentsia:* "collective pl. often with *the.* [Russ. *intelligentsiya.* . . .] Informed intellectual people collectively; the educated or professional group, class or party—often derisive."

The point of all this is that the word, and its ambience, political and social, is really *modern,* having to do with the modern experience. And to that extent it is a problem when the word gets read back into history to describe what seem to be similar phenomena.

The original term *intelligentsia* was Russian. The first use of the word is obscure, but one version has it that it was introduced into the language in the 1860's by a minor novelist named Boborykin—the irony being that the root of the name *boboryk* in Russian means to babble endlessly. Intelligentsia was meant to apply to a generation—that of Belinsky, Chernyshevsky, and others who were becoming critical of society—and it received its definitive stamp in the novel of Turgenev, *Fathers and Sons,* the fathers being the critical thinkers and the sons the nihilists. The formulation is important because it deals with the two aspects that are associated with the idea of an intelligentsia—the primacy of the *ideological* as the focus of its concerns, and a sense of *alienation.* What is implicit in all this is a congerie of moods: the idea of being *engagé,* of being involved in a war of ideas; of being concerned with new and novel ideas; and of detaching oneself from the society of which one is a part.

But the word *intellectual* as a westernization of *intelligentsia,* has a different origin. It arose in France, during the Dreyfus trial. Before that time (1898), the word never seems to have appeared. It was not listed in the *Grand Larousse.* It arose in 1898 in a very curious way. A group of writers, among them Anatole France, Émile Zola, Daniel Halevy, and Marcel Proust, signed a protest asking for a retrial of Captain Dreyfus. It was published in the newspaper *L'Aurore,* and the editor, Georges Clemenceau, gave it the title "Manifesto of the Intellectuals" ("Manifeste des Intellectuels"). They were attacked by a right wing critic, Ferdinand Brunetière:

As for this petition that is being circulated among intellectuals! The mere fact that one has recently created this word intellectuals *to designate, as though they were an aristocracy, individuals who live in laboratories or libraries, proclaims one of the ridiculous eccentricities of our time—I mean the pretension of raising writers, scientists, professors and philologists to the rank of supermen.*

Maurice Barres, also a right wing critic, scorned it as a neologism ("poor French") which applied to the group so typed. The word was used as a battle flag by both sides.

But the decision was turned around, and Dreyfusards such as Clemenceau and Anatole France used it proudly.

In the following year (1899) William James wrote a letter to his brother-in-law referring to the role of the French intellectuals in the Dreyfus affair:

We "intellectuals" in America must all work to keep our precious birthright of individualism, and freedom from those institutions (church, army, aristocracy, royalty). Every great institution is perforce a means of corruption—whatever good it may also do. Only in free personal relation is full ideality to be found.

And as Richard Hofstadter, who quotes that letter, writes:

It is significant in our own history that this early use of the term— the first in America of which I am aware—should have been made in the context of just such a "radical" utopian and anti-institutional statement of purpose.[1]

The word *intellectual* caught on because it crystallized an inchoate comprehension of a new phenomenon. And, to this extent, it is like similar terms such as *alienation, ideology, charisma, identity—* what Raymond Williams called "map-words," in that they draw the outlines of new dimensions of the social world—just as, in the nineteenth century, the world became mapped by words such as *industry, class, democracy,* or in our day, by *bureaucracy, statism, interdependence, externalities,* etc.[2]

As the term spread and became associated with the idea of *intel-*

---

[1] Actually, as Lewis Feuer pointed out in "Ideology and Ideologists, James, in an editorial in *The Nation,* Mar. 1898, deplored Brunetière's sneer at the "intellectuals."

[2] It may even surprise you to know that the word *alienation,* which is so much a cant word of our time, does not even appear in the *Encyclopedia of the Social Sciences,* which came out in 1935. It was even unknown to the first generation of Marxists, such as Plekhanov, Kautsky, Bernstein or Lenin. It appeared in some early works of Marx that were never published in his lifetime, and which appeared only in the 1930's. It is a word of the 1940's and 1950's. *Charisma* came into popular usage in the 1950's, having been employed by a sociologist on *Fortune* to describe John L. Lewis. So new are some of the problems we deal with that if you go to the *International Encyclopedia of the Social Sciences* (a revision of the old Encyclopedia, which came out in 1968) and look up the word *pollution,* you will find: "Pollution is a form of ritual defilement."

The baffled reader, encountering a discussion of taboo, uncleanliness, and the like, may finally realize that it is an article on comparative religion, not on environment and ecology.

lectual activities, more and more confusion arose about what meant by an intellectual—precisely *who* is an intellectual.

If to *be* an intellectual is to be involved in learning, then the historical source of the intellectual is the church, where literacy, learning, and preaching are bound together in a ministry. Over the college gates of Harvard is written:

After God had carried us safe to New England and wee had builded our houses, provided necessaries for our livelihood, rear'd convenient places for God's worship, and settled the Civill Government; One of the new things we longed for, and looked after was to advance Learning, and perpetuate it to posterity; dreading to leave an illiterate Ministry to the Church, when our present Ministers lie in the dust.

So that was the great call. But if the intellectual was the cleric, then he should abstain from mundane affairs. The root of that idea goes back to the distinction formulated by Augustine between the Terrestrial City, which is given up to the Demon and the passion he excites, and the City of God, formed by his servants. From it arose the prescription in canon law: "The Cleric should stand aloof from the Turmoil of temporal affairs."

Not all clerics actually did so, but by and large that was their notion of what a cleric—what an intellectual—should be. He should be absorbed in contemplation, perhaps in theological controversies, but nothing else.

There is an interesting example cited by Bertrand de Jouvenal of a conversation between Eckermann and Goethe. On learning of the July 1830 revolution in France, Eckermann excitedly rushed to see Goethe and found that to Goethe the "great news" was that of Geoffroy Saint-Hilaire's victory over Baron Cuvier in a dispute at the French Academy of Sciences over the transformation of species. (And there is still the question, de Jouvenal has remarked, as to which was the more important event—that, or the revolution of 1830.)

That emphasis on the traditional role of the guardians of learning is central to one of the most famous (and, typically, least read) books of the times, Julien Benda's book, which is translated *The Betrayal of the Intellectuals,* but whose original title in French is *La Trahison Des Clercs,* written in 1927. The book has two themes. It is, first, a defense of intellectualism (cognitive rationalism) against sensibility (feeling) and intuitionism—the enemies being Nietzsche and Bergson. The second is an attack on those intellectuals who have entered the political arena to mobilize *political* hatreds. As Benda wrote, "Our age is indeed the age of the *intellectual organization of political hatreds.* It will be one of its chief claims to notice in the moral history of humanity."

What Benda was saying was that the intellectuals were deserting their traditional role of clerics by providing political formulas to justify and rationalize hatreds—in short, to be *ideologues.* He pointed out that "the clerics originally prevented the layman from setting up their actions as a religion . . . as they carried out these activities. . . . [But] at the end of the 19th century a fundamental change occurred: *The clerks began to play the game of political passions.*"

The intellectuals, one might say, following Benda, had become the priests and prophets of a secular religion and, in so doing, had betrayed their "true" vocation: to defend thought against instinct and intuition; intellectualism against passion, contemplation against action, and universalism against parochialism.[3]

In contemporary sociology the individual who has gone furthest in the direction of seeing the role of the intellectual as a guardian of learning is Edward Shils. He has written:

In every society . . . there are some persons with an unusual sensitivity to the sacred, *an uncommon reflectiveness about the nature of their universe, and the rules which govern their society. There is in every society a minority of persons who, more than the ordinary run of their fellow men, are enquiring, and desirous of being in frequent* communion *with symbols, which are more general than the immediate concrete situations of everyday life, and* remote *in their references in both time and space. In this minority there is a need to externalize this quest in oral and written discourse, in poetic or plastic expression, in historical reminiscence and acts of worship. This interior need to penetrate beyond the screen of immediate concrete experiences marks the existence of the intellectuals in every society. (Italics mine.)*

[3] Paradoxically, it was two French Jews that led the opposing sides: Henri Bergson in flaunting intuitionism, and Benda in defending intellectualism.

If I make roman the key words in this quotation, here is a view which stresses the sacred, communion, remoteness, and acts of worship as comprising the vocation of the intellectual.

Yet if now one looks at a contemporary society, if in some way we associate intellectuals not only with expressive symbols, but also with knowledge, we suddenly veer almost 180 degrees from that direction. For as knowledge becomes more complex, more technical, and more specialized, a new role—and a new person—arises: the intellectual expert, the one who in contemporary terms comes closest to what Bickerman would have called the scribes—the ones who provide counsel, general ideas, or interpret the specialized knowledge to the rulers and policy-makers. Much of this work—of economists, of political scientists, of physicists or engineers—is journeyman's work, no different within its realm than an artisan working within his craft. Yet at the higher reaches of policy, there is a class of persons one would call intellectuals, especially where one has to mix normative questions and technical issues to provide solutions or answers to problems. In this country, that class goes back to the days of Woodrow Wilson, who first brought "intellectuals" into government. It received a large impetus during Roosevelt's New Deal, when a well-publicized "brain trust" was created to cope with the Depression. Since then the process has been institutionalized in the Council of Economic Advisors, The Domestic Policy Council, The National Security Advisors—and we have the obvious personae in Kissinger, Bundy, Rostow, *et al.* in foreign affairs, or Walter Heller, Paul Samuelson, Milton Friedman *et al.* in the economic realm. In contradistinction to the intellectual as the man of passion, or the intellectual as transcendental intellect, we have the intellectual as the man concerned with relevant policy.

I have gone into this history, and to this typology, to illustrate the difficulty of talking about "The Intellectual in American Society." What does one mean?

In one sense, all three kinds of intellectuals have been present in American society. True, the concern with the "sacred" (even the secular sacred, i.e. the civil religion) is probably the rarest, though the earliest. In that respect, the Puritans were the earliest examples of our intellectuals, though there is a paradox, of course, in that the

Puritans were strongly anti-institutional and anti-antinomian: society was corrupt. One had to return to the primitive simplicity of the original church which drew its will directly from God rather than from man-made institutions.

Yet the great figures of Puritanism were certainly intellectuals, and it is striking that Jonathan Edwards, the strictest of Calvinists, who also became the first President of what is now Princeton, was the exemplar for Van Wyck Brooks of the "highbrow" (when Brooks wrote *America's Coming of Age* in 1915, he coined the distinction of highbrow and lowbrow: Benjamin Franklin was the lowbrow and Jonathan Edwards was the highbrow) and drew from those two the subsequent lineaments of American intellectual history.

It is striking—and a subject for meditation—that there is probably no one today in American intellectual life who represents that kind of intellectual. The last, perhaps, a man who in his own way bridged all three types, though he derived his strength so completely from the interpretation of the sacred, particularly in its Augustinian sense, was Reinhold Niebuhr. But since then we have had none.

Of the nature and problem of the policy intellectuals—and the complex relations of truth to power, the classic issue for such men— we are, or I should say, I am, too close to the scene to have the necessary distance to establish a perspective, let alone a judgment.

So, for my discussion of "the" intellectual in American society— after this long excursis—I will speak of what might be called the "intelligentsia." And therefore I am simply taking one of the three different types—in part to illustrate a process about America. And I will concentrate, because of the intrinsic fascination of the group, on The New York Jewish intelligentsia, *c.* 1935-65.

One initial premise has to be understood. It makes little sense to talk of "the" intellectual and "the society," or even "the" artist and "the society." Some individuals are truly great and their work, in a transcendent sense, takes on a meaning beyond their time. But as a social phenomena, as a *genus,* there is no "single" intellectual, but a collectivity. Intellectuals are *like-minded* persons, united around a set of ideas and passions, who seek to promote them. They do so through manifestos, by founding magazines, by creating clubs—and it is as a *collectivity* (despite large individual differences) that one locates and understands them in relation to a time. In short, between the individual and the society is a mediating instrument—and by some odd linguistic quirk I do not understand, almost all the words one wants to use to describe this begin with the letter *c*: coterie, clique, circle, cenacle, club, college, chapel, curia, etc. (I have actually found twenty-seven words to describe these small entities—and in passing, you may now know the esoteric element behind *The Cultural Contradictions of Capitalism*. It comes out of my theory of small *c*'s.)

An intelligentsia, therefore, is a collectivity which comes together and represents a commonality—often they come from some common milieu and seek for common meanings. They seek to explore their own *lives* for the way those meanings express their lives, but also symbolize some larger group of which they are a part. And, under conditions of conflict, they may become ideologues or shapers of identity.

The first group of this sort we find in American life appeared in New York, roughly around 1912, and, curiously enough, they called themselves, self-consciously, "The Young Intellectuals." The noun was taken over from Europe; it was meant to signify, as it did to the Marxists, the young members of the bourgeois class who had repudiated that class. But more than that; it was also, self-consciously, the "young men from the Provinces"—the Julien Sorels or Rastignacs who had come to the Capitol to become cosmopolitan. In all it was a very impressive group: from Harvard there were Walter Lippmann, Van Wyck Brooks, John Reed; from Yale, Waldo Frank, Sinclair Lewis, Paul Rosenfeld, Archibald MacLeish; from Princeton, Edmund Wilson, F. Scott Fitzgerald.

What united them was the protest against the genteel tradition, the domination of America by the small town and the crabbed respectability which the small town was enforcing. What enthralled them was the teeming vibrancy of urban ethnic life. What attracted them was an exuberance summed up in a series of catchwords. One of them was "new"—the New Democracy, the New Nationalism, the New Poetry—even the *New Republic,* which was started in 1914. A second was "sex," a word which used openly to proclaim a sexual revolution; and the word sex sent a *frisson* through the rest of the society. And the third was the word *liberation*. Liberation, which the movement self-consciously ascribed to itself, was the wind blowing from Europe, the wind of Modernism come to the American shore— such as that symbolized by the Fauves and Cubism in the Armory show of 1913. And the favorite "doctrine of the Rebellion," as Henry May has written, was that happiness would follow complete instinctual self-expression. The intellectual avatars of the group were Nietzsche, Freud, and Henry Bergson (whose doctrine of vitalism—that of a biological purposive spirit which animated the universe—was a best-seller). Politically, these children of rebellion were attached to the I.W.W. and its swashbuckling spirit, and social and political rebels (such as Big Bill Haywood) mingled freely in the salons of Greenwich Village.

What killed the "Rebellion" was first World War I—which was supported, surprisingly, by a large proportion of the intellectuals and led to the famous acerbic essay by Randolph Bourne, "The War and the Intellectuals":

. . . it has been a bitter experience to see the unanimity with which American intellectuals have thrown their support to the use of war-technique in the crisis. Socialists, college professors, publicists, new-republicans, practitioners of literature, have vied with each other in confirming with their intellectual faith the collapse of neutrality and the riveting of the war-mind on a hundred million more of the world's people. And the intellectuals are not content with confirming our belligerent gesture. They are now complacently asserting that it was they who willed it, against the hesitation and dim perceptions of the American democratic masses. A war made deliberately by the intellectuals!

The second element, after the war, was, ironically, the "New Capitalism." American capitalism had taken on a new lease on life, and, perhaps in unconscious mockery of the new freedom of the intellectuals, it called its unrestrained appetite the "New Capitalism."

The surging prosperity of America after the war, the victory of the Babbitts and the "Booboisie," drove the young intellectuals abroad. And in the 1920's we have the famous "lost generation" of literary expatriates—from the Hemingways and the Fitzgeralds to the dozens and dozens of smaller lights whose memories and autobiographies now fill whole walls of American Studies alcoves—who gave some romantic memories and effulgent years to what the best and worst of them called "A Moveable Feast."

What is striking about these two generations is that, despite some overlap, the "Greenwich Village intellectuals" of the pre-war years and the Paris expatriates of the 1920's represented, for the first time, distinct collectivities who could be called "intelligentsia." Among the Paris expatriates were those who were attracted by the excitement and novelty of the experimental arts—of modernism—then of political radicalism, and in other times would have been more like dandies than intellectuals. But one cannot compare sociological types in formal terms. Historical events and consciousness had intervened. The Rebellion of the 1920's lived off the memory of World War I and the shattering of any mere aesthetic life. And therefore there was an inevitable political tinge to it, even when most of its energies, such as those devoted to the literary magazines, went primarily into esthetic experimentation.

What is left to be explained—and this is far outside the scope of this paper—is why there were so few "intelligentsia" movements in the United States, and why they were by and large, unlike those of Europe, largely of the Left.

There is a myth—which itself requires explanation—that the "intelligentsia" in the West has been identified so strongly with the Left. (The easy explanation is that the Left won so completely after World War II, and in the subsequent decade and a half it became so substantially the war between the communists and the social democrats, often allied with the excommunists.)

Yet in Europe in the 1920's the major literary and cultural figures in most countries were of the Right—Pound, Wyndham Lewis, Yeats, Eliot in the Anglo-Saxon world; Stefan George, Ernest Friedrich Junger, Gottfried Benn in Germany; Maumas, Daudet, Mauriac, Bernanos in France; Marinetti, d'Annunzio, Pirandello in Italy. What was striking about these figures was the degree to which they championed cultural modernism (through its emphasis on experimentalism) with its distaste for bourgeois sensibility.

In the United States there was one other collectivity of intellectuals—those identified as the Southern Agrarians, originating in Vanderbilt University, whose ideas were featured in a famous manifesto, "I'll Take My Stand." The group was almost entirely literary and symbolized by such figures as Allan Tate, Robert Penn Warren, Cleanth Brooks, John Crowe Rawsonn, Donald Davidson, and the

like. Yet what they were defending, they felt, was an agrarian way of
life, the rhythms of a gentler time and quieter place—and with it a
mode of aristocratic learning which would take the word as the text
and ignore the mundane biographical, sociological, or other appurte-
nances to the exegesis of meaning other than the Logos above. They
were intellectuals of "spirit"—of courtliness and repose—and the
chroniclers of the passions of blood and menstrual sex, but while
they dealt with ideas and passions, curiously, they eschewed politics—
at least in the eschatalogical and gnostic meanings which have been
at the esoteric heart the creeds of all of the "intelligentsia."

   We come now, finally, to the heart of my subject, the New York
Jewish Intellectuals (c. 1930-65). Who they were I have indicated in
the accompanying genealogy.

The New York Jewish Intellectuals
c. 1935—c. 1965

1. *The Elders: Coming of Age in the late 1920's and early 1930's*

Elliot Cohen	Lionel Trilling	Hannah Arendt†
Sidney Hook	Meyer Schapiro	Diana Trilling
Philip Rahv	William Phillips	

Gentile Cousins: Max Eastman   Fred Dupee
                   Edmund Wilson   Dwight Macdonald
                   Reinhold Niebuhr   James T. Farrell

The "Other Synagogue."   Michael Gold   Joseph Freeman

Magazines: *Menorah Journal, The New Masses, Partisan Review*

1. A. *The Younger Brothers: Coming of Age in the mid and late 1930's*

Alfred Kazin	Harold Rosenberg
Richard Hofstadter	Clement Greenberg
Saul Bellow*	Lionel Abel
Delmore Schwartz	Paul Goodman
Bernard Malamud	Issac Rosenfeld

European Relatives: Nicola Chiaramonte   George Lichtheim

Gentile Cousins: Mary McCarthy   William Barrett
                   Elizabeth Hardwick   Richard Chase
                   James Baldwin   Ralph Ellison
                   Arthur Schlesinger, Jr.

Magazines: *The Nation, The New Republic, Partisan Review, Commentary, Politics*

2. *The Second Generation: Coming of Age in the late 1930's and early 1940's*

Daniel Bell	Irving Kristol
Irving Howe	Melvin Lasky
Leslie Fiedler*	Nathan Glazer
Robert Warshow	S. M. Lipset*
Gertrude Himmelfarb	David Bazelon

Gentile Cousins: Murray Kempton   C. Wright Mills

Magazines: *Commentary, Partisan Review, Encounter,* *The New Leader, Dissent, The Public Interest*

2. A. *The Younger Brothers: Coming of Age in the late 1940's and early 1950's*

Norman Podhoretz	Jason Epstein	Norman Mailer
Steven Marcus	Robert Silvers	Philip Roth
Robert Brustein	Susan Sontag	
Midge Decter	Theo. Solotaroff	

Gentile Cousins: Michael Harrington   "The Paris Review"‡

Magazines: *Commentary, Partisan Review, New York Review of Books*

The European Intelligentsia

Raymond Aron	Jean-Paul Sartre
Arthur Koestler	Albert Camus
Ignazio Silone	Simone de Beauvior
George Orwell	
Manes Sperber	
Davud Rousset	

The English Intelligentsia

Isaiah Berlin
Stuart Hampshire
Stephen Spender
Noel Annan
John Gross
Jonathan Miller

Institutional Attachments

Columbia University
Congress for Cultural Freedom

Influentials—at a distance
         T. S. Eliot   Robert Lowell   Edward Shils
         W. H. Auden   James Agee

† Arrived later, yet became one of the elders.
* Outside New York but had status as members.
‡ The social and intellectual coterie that included George Plimpton, William Styron.

The New York Jewish Intellectuals
(by field of interest)

Art: Meyer Schapiro, Clement Greenberg, Harold Rosenberg

Philosophy: Sidney Hook, Hannah Arendt (Ernest Nagel)

Literary Criticism: Lionel Trilling, Philip Rahv, Alfred Kazin, Irving Howe, Leslie Fiedler, Paul Goodman, Lionel Abel, Steven Marcus, Robert Warshow, Robert Brustein, Susan Sontag, Diana Trilling

Intellectual Journalism: Elliot Cohen, William Phillips, Irving Kristol, Melvin Lasky, Robert Silvers, Norman Podhoretz, Jason Epstein, Theodore Solotaroff, Midge Decter

Poetry: Delmore Schwartz

Fiction: Saul Bellow, Bernard Malamud, Norman Mailer, Isaac Rosenfeld, Philip Roth (Harvey Swados)

Theology: (Will Herberg) (Emil Fackenheim) (Jacob Taubes) (Arthur Cohen)

Sociology: Daniel Bell, Nathan Glazer, S. M. Lipset, (Philip Selznick) (Edward Shils) (Lewis Coser)

History: Richard Hofstadter, Gertrude Himmelfarb (Arthur Schlesinger, Jr.)
Economics: (Robert Heilbroner) (Robert Lekachman)

NOTE: Parentheses indicate individuals who were close enough at times to be regarded as writers who could be "cousins."

There are many extraordinary things one can say about these extraordinary people, but what I shall attempt to say—and I trust that I am not misunderstood—is that this group, within its short generational span, encapsulated in the most surprising way two of the complex features which summed up American cultural life in the thirty-five-year period—the union of political radicalism and cultural modernism; and while, in their early years, they had hoped to flee America (what happened, though, both in the late 1930's and in

World War II, is that "Europe" came here), in the end they inherited the cultural establishment of America in ways that they—and certainly their fathers—could never have dreamed of.

At this point let me go back to a bit of terminology and theory. In order to understand the way in which intellectuals think of themselves as intellectuals—not necessarily in pejorative or non-pejorative terms—one must recognize that the touchstone of what concerns them is *the idea of experience*. Tradition, authority, revelation, or reason as modes of knowledges are available to *all* men. But *common experience* is available only to a small number who have been deeply touched by the event, and with those with whom they can share an emotional bond. This is why the idea of a *generation* becomes such a singular sociological entity and why as a symbolic term it provides a common entelechy and a common bond for persons. Because that awareness arises in youth, many persons come to think of themselves largely in youth and generational terms. To that extent, it becomes a very real rupture in the character of culture and tradition. If you ask a person in a traditional society, Who are you? The answer is clear. I am Ivan Petrovitch, I am Ahmed Ben Ali, I am John Thompson—in effect, I am the son of my father, and the patronymic is given as the mode of response. In the modern temper, one says that *I* am *I*. I come out of myself. And one searches out others who have had experiences like one's own. And these people find one another.

It is a great mystery, and I do not know any historian or sociologist who is able to explain it, but at certain times and in certain places, such a coterie, clique, cenacle somehow comes together, crystallizes, and coalesces as an entity in this particular way. And this entity becomes an identity. One finds this in an extraordinary number of places: in Budapest just before World War I, in Bloomsbury in the 1910's, in Paris and Vienna in the 1920's, in Oxford in the 1930's—and in New York in the 1940's. These New York Jewish intellectuals came together as a self-conscious group, knowing each other, writing primarily for each other, discussing ideas they held in common, differing widely and sometimes savagely, and yet having that sense of kinship which made each of them aware that they were part of a distinctive socio-historical phenomenon.

And yet, in trying to find out about such a group, one runs up against an extraordinary problem—a problem of sources. Very little has been published—memoirs, letters, personal essays—which provides documentation for the intellectual vagaries of the group. In this connection it is curious to look at two other phenomena. One is the recent New Left. An extraordinary fact of sociological life is the extent of instant history that was created with the New Left. There are today probably dozens and dozens of memoirs, histories, collections of manifestos, documents, picture books, biographies—you name them—which deal with the New Left. The remainder tables of Harvard Square bookstores are full of them. The second is the phenomenon of the Beats—persons like Allan Ginsberg or Jack Kerouac or Lawrence Ferlinghetti or William Burroughs, who appear endlessly in each others' novels, in articles about their novels, and in the media events describing their parties and performances.

Of the intelligentsia of the 1960's and 1950's, we are flooded with miles of words—and they are worthless. Postured, posed, self-stereo-typed. Of the New York Jewish intellectuals, I only know one account, and that is the book by Norman Podhoretz called *Making It* (which, when it appeared, embarrassed all his friends), and, earlier, three novels, one almost entirely unknown, by Tess Slessinger, called *The Unpossessed,* which is largely about the *Menorah Journal,* the group around Eliot Cohen in the late 1920's and early 1930's, and ten years later, Mary McCarthy's kiss-and-tell novels, *The Company She Keeps* and *The Oasis.*

How can we explain this? The New Left was in part a media event, and therefore it had a self-consciousness about its own posturing. The Beats were narcissistic, and their experiments, in drugs or homosexuality, quickly attracted the view of the would-be voyeurs. But about the New York intellectuals, the fifty within the inner group, or several hundred of the others, there are almost no memoirs, no biographical accounts, no reflections which try to explain their lives. And even when there are one or two, such as Irving Howe's account of the phenomenon, it is about the characteristics of the *style* of the group, not of their lives as persons.

I think there are two reasons for this. One is that almost all of these individuals come out of themselves. They had no *yichus*.[4] The background of all of these men was largely immigrant, their parents

[4] Yiddish for "eminent pedigree."

themselves working class or petty bourgeois who had led rather drab, rather uneventful lives. And in an extraordinary way, difficult as it is to deal with, there was a sense of shame about the differences between themselves and their parents. So it became difficult somehow to discuss their origins, and it got all pushed away. Second, there was a pride in the group that what was important were really *ideas* and one should not talk about people as celebrities. Ideas were passionately and fiercely debated and therefore one would not, even among intimate friends (and I have lived among the group most of my life), ask about family background or where one came from. What was there to tell?

I think that the very nature of their limited backgrounds indicates that what really animated and drove them was a hunger for culture. In a sense, going to college could be called a conversion to culture, coming out of slum or ghetto background and finding a whole world open that we had never known before. Here is Podhoretz talking about his days at Columbia, which was true to some extent as well about the early generation at City College:

Though our main interest lay in literature, we scorned the scholarly journals like PMLA [Proceedings of the Modern Language Association]. *On the other hand, we read the literary magazines religiously, in particular* Partisan Review *and* Kenyon Review. *Moreover, we thought of ourselves not as Americans or Jews, but as novitiates of the Republic of Letters, a world of whose concrete physical existence we had less doubt than about the existence of the Midwest. Our Republic included everyone who had ever been instrumental in shaping Western civilization. Herodotus and St. Augustine, D. H. Lawrence and Yeats were all equally distinguished members of the community which we aspired to join. And we conceived of this community in space rather than in time. Despite the fact that we sat at the feet of Lionel Trilling, our sense of history was underdeveloped. Like Mortimer Adler—a Columbia graduate who never grew out of the idea—we saw a "great conversation" going on everlastingly between authors remote from one another in time, space, interest, and intention. We saw them all sitting around a great conference table, discussing the same problems, and always lining up on the same sides. It was the unity of culture, not the differences, that appealed most to our imagination.*

Along with this went a great Anglophilia. England was a home-
land because it was the country of manners and sensibilities. It is no
accident, I suppose, that the best writings of Trilling are those on
Matthew Arnold or E. M. Forster or Jane Austin, because that was
the kind of life—a life of manners, a life of society, a life of culture
which gave a great sense of coherent social structure or of nuanced
relationships.

We thought that we would be the heirs of sensibility, the heirs, in
effect, of what the *modern* was all about. There was with it an intellectual radicalism, a radicalism which came from the reading of Marx
and Freud, the emphasis on the social conditions of literature itself.
And there was a repudiation of religion. Some were *apikorsim*,[5] those
who knew something and rebelled; but most were *am-horatzim*[6] those
who simply had no knowledge of tradition. But for both the style of
life which was appealing was cosmopolitan.

It is also important to note that there were economic circumstances which tend to explain so much of this—the fact of the Depression. If one looks at the careers of many of these people, their prospects were quite precarious. Sidney Hook and Ernest Nagel began
teaching in high school, Dick Hofstadter in evening college, and Lionel Trilling, because of the anti-Semitism at Columbia, stayed on by
the bare chance of the intervention of Nicholas Murray Butler. Many
of them had odd jobs. Harold Rosenberg, the art critic of the *New
Yorker*, worked on WPA. Clement Greenberg our other great art
critic, began as a customs guard. Melvin Lasky, the editor of *Encounter*, worked at the Statue of Liberty. (To our great envy, he had
passed an exam as junior historical archivist and was given a job of
telling the chance visitor the history of the statue.) My colleague Irving Kristol worked as a machinist in the Brooklyn Navy Yard. Many
others, luckily, had working wives who taught in the elementary
schools of New York, so they could be supported while they wrote
their esoteric essays.

There was a very real sense of exclusion from America. The classic
story is that of Elliot Cohen, the founding editor of *Commentary*.
Elliot Cohen was probably one of the brightest students Yale Uni-

[5] "Atheist," a Talmudic word derived from Epicurus, but meaning "intellectual
renegade"; it came into modern Yiddish.
[6] A Yiddish plural for ignorant or illiterate; the singular is *am ho-oretz*.

versity had had in many years. He had a great passion and devotion to English literature, and his chief desire was to teach English there. Yet he was told by one of the great figures there, "Mr. Cohen, you are a very distinguished scholar. But it is hard for me to imagine a Hebrew, teaching the Protestant tradition to young men at Yale." (It is quite striking that one of the great luminaries in the English Department at Yale today is Harold Bloom, who has just written a marvelous book called *Kabbalah and Criticism*.)

In effect, there was an ideological stance of alienation, and in an extraordinary way this was summed up in an essay by Thorstein Veblen, written in the 1920's, in which he described what he felt was Jewish spirit:

. . . In short, he is a skeptic by force of circumstances over which he has no control. . . . Intellectually he is likely to become an alien; spiritually he is more than likely to remain a Jew; for the heartstrings of affection and consuetude are tied early, and they are not readily retied in after life. Nor does the animus with which the community of safe and sane Gentiles is wont to meet him conduce at all to his personal incorporation in that community, whatever may befall the intellectual assets which he brings. Their people need not become his people nor their gods his gods, and indeed the provocation is forever and irritably present all over the place to turn back from following after them. . . . One who goes away from home will come to see many unfamiliar things, and to take note of them; but it does not follow that he will swear by all the strange gods whom he meets along the road.

And there was an essay written more than thirty years ago by a young man whom I once knew very well, which also tried to sum up this thought. That writer said, in an essay in *The Jewish Frontier:*

Jewish living can best be understood by comprehending each individual's need for love and the crucial role of love in Western religious experience. In Catholicism, the church is an agency for winning love and salvation, its tolerant forgiveness through confessional the healing salve for sin. Among the Protestants each man can lean upon God directly and through that grace reach love. In Jewish life the cradle of love is the family. It is more primitive and tribal, yet more direct and intimate than any other creed. It is also, in our time, the most painful. For the heritage of each Jew is the loss of home and the destiny of footsore wandering. The story of the Prodigal Son, thus, is ever alive. But it is more meaningful and real today, for the Prodigal Son's return can rarely be realized. The Jew values the quality of sacrifice which characterized that home, yet he knows that two languages, not one, are spoken, and the sons cannot speak to the elders.

In the Catholic world, one can leave one's home and wander in various fields, but the tents of the Church are large, its compassion great, forgiveness easy. The loss of home in Protestant living is more difficult, yet not shattering, for each man is still part of the entire community who are bound by an impersonal ethic of love. But in Jewish life, each home is an island unto itself, and the severing of the ties of family and tradition causes a tremor which can never be settled. The position of the Jews through the centuries, a stranger in every land, no voice, no ban their own, deepens this traumatic condition. For not only have they no home as their own as a people, but within each alien culture the strange gods tear away the sons and there is no home in the family.

The young Jew is left helpless, and aware. He is aware of a distance both from the Jewish culture from which he came and the Gentile culture into which he cannot or will not enter. He is helpless, for he cannot find his roots in either. Yet out of this tension of understanding and inhibition has bred a new kind of Jew, the Jew of alienation, a Jew who consciously accepts this situation and utilizes his alienation to see, as if through a double set of glasses, each blending their perspective into one, the nature of the tragedy of our time.

Now that, I think, perhaps sums up the mood of what this immigrant generation was about.

There is a longer story, which is the particular history of this generation: namely its attraction to political radicalism in the 1930's and its break with communism, a break which came in large part because of the Moscow trials, by which a whole generation of old Bolsheviks were murdered, or the episodes in Spain, where the G.P.U. slaughtered numbers of left wing persons, an episode that was written about later by George Orwell in *Homage to the Catalonia*. The notion that the Soviet Union, which had promised freedom, was incarcerating millions of its people in concentration camps—the Gulag Archipelago, or the Slansky trials in Czechoslovakia, the Rajk trials in Hungary, and, finally, the beginning of wholesale waves of anti-Semitism, the Doctor's plot, which was beginning to signal a new purge, a move that was cut short by Stalin's death—all created a disillusionment that became final.

At bottom, however, all this posed the oldest of all problems underlying politics. Was what was going on in Russia rooted largely in Russian history? Or was it the unrestrained expression of man as *homo duplex:* the creative which has the impulse to love yet equally an impulse to murder? Does one explain the Soviet Union by history or theology? For many of us, the answer lay not in history, but in the nature of man. It was the end of a belief in much of Marxism. The fact that this opportunity to murder arises when a man is unrestrained by law became an important consideration in the thoughts of those who began a return to Judaism.

The return to Judaism itself, it seems to me, is quite complex. It took form in a unique way. Most of this generation was not Zionist, because there was no sense that Zion or Israel itself was a place that one could attach one's self to. This generation had grown up in *galut,* "exile," and would spend its life there. But a sense of Jewish identity came out of a return to a *particularism,* and one which lived in tension with the *universalism* which had once been sought. It is that tension between universalism and particularism which seems to me has been the historical stance, emotionally and intellectually, of that generation.

After World War II a whole series of events brought that generation into the society very quickly, giving them respected places in universities, publishing houses, and magazines, and in effect allowing many to become some of the brightest stars in American culture itself. A decade ago, that intellectual generation began to break up. The reasons are complex: some of it was the Cold War, some the contrasting reaction to youth in the 1960's; for some there was continuing appeal of modernism, for others a retreat to more traditional elements.

That history, itself deep and complex, would require a very different lecture. But I use this story to indicate one process—namely, that though it was important for that generation, as it is for most intellectual generations, to find its own identity, the real desire was to find a *home*. But whether that home can have a rooted meaning is another question—especially when one lives, recurrently, in the tension of the parochial and the universal.

Today there is no New York Jewish intelligentsia; there is no Jewish intellectual community. Typically, the Owl of Minerva flies at dusk and knowledge is discovered too late. In the period of its decline American society has discovered the Jewish writer, be he Saul Bellow or Bernard Malamud or Philip Roth or critics such as Harold Rosenberg who write for magazines such as *Commentary, The New York Review of Books*. But that no longer reflects any community; these are only broken fragments reflecting their own diffuse current anxieties over the precarious character of American society.

Now, in trying to define the intellectual, I presented, in one sense, three tableaus: the intellectual in relation to the sacred, as a guardian of learning; the intellectual as expert, as a professional (without going into this at all); and the intellectual as a critic or ideologue. The ideological impulse in this country, even though it has been couched in bitter words of criticism, paradoxically, has been a hunger for inclusion, whether it be that of "The Young Intellectuals" of sixty years ago or that of the Jewish intellectuals of thirty years ago. Curiously perhaps, the only two movements today which are ideological, the blacks and Women's Liberation, in their own ways resemble the movements of the earlier periods in that combination of criticism with a desire for inclusion. However revolutionary the rhetoric, then and now, the action belie the words.

What is most striking, if one thinks of intellectuals in the broad sociological context, is the incredible growth today of the professional class, which is a product of a post-industrial society. The professional class is the largest of its kind in human history. There has been an extraordinary expansion in the number of scientists, economists, businessmen, educators, etc., yet little vitality. The reason is that that kind of intellectual—and this is his strength—is primarily instrumental. One can have a technique, one becomes a professional. Yet in the nature of their activities, they cannot seek for the larger moral and prophetic perspectives which intellectuals in the past have striven for.

About the sacred, which is the deepest current of all, for the moment one can only say there is silence. Oddly, there is one place in the world where the tradition of an intelligentsia as a critical opposition fused with the sacred does exist. It is in the Soviet Union. If poets are, as Rimbaud once said, *voyants,* the far-seeing persons of the times, who in their quivering and quaking anticipate the tremors to come, then in the Soviet Union, as we have seen, the underground dissident and submerged voices are largely religious, a cry for a faith which is redemptive of the present.

It may well be that great travails bring forth, in the end, great leaps of faith. And one does not wish for one's own country the travails which provoke the call of *Eli, Eli.* Yet the storms are coming, storms which derive from the mundane failure to manage a complex society, from the loss of confidence in a national will, from the erosion of legitimacy and the authority of institutions such as the universities, which have failed to be what they were intended to be—an Establishment. But economic and political questions apart, what is lacking, at bottom, is a moral coherence, which comes from a sense that a place in the world necessarily involves a transcendent tie and a transcendental obligation. In a world where the intellectual class is either largely utilitarian or instrumental, or where the intellectual class and its culture is largely anti-institutional and antinomian, then no vision is possible; and that is the bleak future of an American culture and its intellectual class.

The subject here is "Tomorrow's American," and I have spoken almost entirely of the past. Yet clearly one can only know tomorrow if one understands the past. Within a national context, an intellectual is one who seeks to articulate the national purpose—and this was the extraordinary role of such persons as Jefferson, Mazzini, and Masaryk. And clearly it is easier to articulate that purpose at the founding of a nation than at its decline. There is a decline—as I have argued in "The End of American Exceptionalism," in the Fall 1975 *Public Interest*—in large measure because of the *hubris* of the country in seeking to take on the role of a world power and imperial eminence that it could not—either by national style or for the lack of a ruthless will—and that may well have been its saving grace, because we could not, as did the Russians, trample down a Hungary or a Czechoslovakia, and even though we bombarded Vietnam, we still held back from the final *Schrecklichkeit* of obliterating it completely.

But I suppose, apart from this *hubris,* the essential sociological point is that we are a *nation,* but not a *community.* We may not become a community, until we include, not by assimilation, but by pluralism, all partial communities into a *comity* of communities. But we are finding that this is not easy. The voices of rage rise higher—as in the last decade—over the voices of moderation; or, as in this moment, we live in a state of emotional exhaustion over our problems.

The immediate problems are economic and political, but as in any society, the root problems are cultural and moral, since these make legitimate our actions and purposes. Those who began this country made a political revolution—a curious one, for it was entirely political, not social, as in France or, later, in Russia, to rework the entire social structure of the country. It was a political revolution in the demand for liberty, yet it was a revolution within a transcendental frame, and that frame gave it vision and drive. Today, there is no transcendental frame—no sense of what is sacred and what is profane—and without that distinction, without *havdolah,*[7] the world becomes an endless routine, with no marking points of meaning. That is the problem of today. It is, by that very fact, the problem of Tomorrow's America.

---

7 "Distinction," originally that between the sacred and the profane, or between the Sabbath and the rest of the week. Literally, "separation of realms."

III

EDWARD A.
PATRICK, M.D., Ph.D

MEDICAL SCIENCE

AND

FOREWORD

Ladies and gentlemen, tonight I am most pleased to give this, the
third of the Weil Lectures in observance of America's Bicentennial.
It is a privilege to be asked to follow or precede such distinguished
speakers. At the outset I regret omitting those subjects from the medical sciences which will not be discussed tonight. I appreciate your
willingness to hear my views on Tomorrow's American 200 years
from now.

Two weeks ago I came from Indiana to hear one of the other
speakers in this Weil Lecture series. I sat in the back row next to a
lady who had with her a newspaper with the pictures of all the

Tomorrow's American

speakers. She pointed to mine and said, "My, isn't Dr. Patrick young!" It was very flattering to hear her say that, until she added, "But for all I know he might be seventy." Even though I am only about half that age, I suppose I am over the hill; but I cannot worry very much about it, knowing all the work going on to replace aging organs with plastic.

In any case, the United States is young, as are those medical frontiers which will affect Americans in 200 years. Most such frontiers developed over only the last few decades. Because of many other unforeseen frontiers, I will be myopic in viewing the effect of medical sciences on Tomorrow's American. Still, by exploring areas of basic research along with the country's needs, we can see both short-term and long-term possible advances.

INTRODUCTION

Tomorrow's American will be profoundly influenced by the developing medical sciences, but also by developments in what some still consider foreign areas: computers, physics, space science, engineering, and society itself. Despite advances, some current health care problems will remain. For example, the individual's need for considerate, quality attention to his health problems will never disappear. The primary provider, that is, the doctor whom you go to see first, may not be a family physician, but that will be determined both by the levels of public intelligence and technology achieved.

Just as we have expanded the role for family physicians and nurse practitioners during the past five years, we will turn to a new specialty of diagnosis and treatment during the next ten years as the need for additional family physicians decreases. Just as we have developed and described surgical procedures for diseases during the past fifty years, we will learn to integrate engineering developments and the computer into surgery. And just as we have learned to describe and treat mental disease through psychiatry, we will learn to teach the public quality mental health and individual responsibilty, derived from psychiatric and psychological principles.

I am not going to tell you science fiction, nor am I a psychic. Rather, there are some fundamentals of technological assessment or forecasting, itself an emerging science, which can be applied. There are, of course, pitfalls in forecasting. Consider that our law of gravity was discovered only 400 years ago. A new concept of gravity could change the economics of space flights and space colonization. Considering that the cell's microstructure based on DNA and RNA was only recently discovered, the genetic engineering we think of today for modifying intelligence or interrupting cancer growth must be very primitive. Our Viking landing on Mars, scheduled for about July 4, 1976, could find new forms of life or new materials which would open up a new area of medical advances. Of the eleven materials in use in 8000 B.C., only two, wood and stone, remain in significant use in today's society.

Thus, it is likely that I will underpredict advances as far away as 200 years, but overpredict the near future. For the first time in history there are rapid new advances coming from engineering, engineering sciences, physics, and space ventures which will affect health care. For example, the same electronic circuits in modern communications and the same control principles used in space navigation are now being used in artificial limbs and in devices to assist the failing human heart.

LIMITED RESOURCES AND PLANNING

We must face the possibility that medicine might allow a certain population to survive now, through exhausting resources, at the reduction in the amount of future life.

Scientists and the United States Government are making some progress in planning to prevent such a crisis. For example, a science office has once again been established in the White House, and panels are being formed to examine contributions of technology to economic strength and what advances in science and technology may have an impact on national policy in the next decade.

Unfortunately, there appear to be no specific plans to examine how scientific and technological advances may affect health care in America. Instead, a second advisory group is being proposed; a National Health Council affiliated with the Department of Health, Education, and Welfare would advise the President and Congress on health care delivery. This separation of science and engineering from health care is not best at a time when many of the emerging components which will affect tomorrow's health care systems are coming from science or engineering.

A third government organization to study our future is the Office of Technology Assessment, which became active in 1974 as a result of the Technology Assessment Act of 1972. They also appear to have a "hands-off" attitude toward health care delivery.

A fourth organization is NASA, which is funding research in medical engineering. Probably there were few direct medical applications from space programs, except for the education of engineers and technicians who are available now to work on health care problems. But the indirect contributions have been many. In my opinion, future space ventures will provide great opportunity for direct contributions to health care.

America's present method of funding research and development through the National Institutes of Health, the National Science Foundation, NASA, and the military is no longer acceptable for health care research, especially that involving engineering and medicine. It may have functioned during the industrial age just past, but will not today. For example, the time constant for change in hospitals was very large compared with that in industry. For this reason and others, engineering schools have been geared to train engineers for industry. University education was not concerned with hospitals. Finally, however, engineering had to have an impact on the hospital as is happening today. The hospitals are just emerging from a pre-industrial age into an industrial age. As the time constant for change continues to decrease for the hospital, it will have to exercise sharp short- and long-term planning in order to remain efficient and of high quality.

Most hospitals have not been oriented to perform research and development of new systems for health care delivery. Several major hospitals now are proceeding in that direction. A major hospital should have a division for research and development, possibly in collaboration with university engineering departments and conventional industry. This division would have both short-term and long-term goals; it would have in-house, private, and government funding. Such a research division would be to the President's health care council just as an industrial research division was and is to military developments. Americans, decide: do you want health care advances to approach military advances, even just a little?

Long before the year 2176 there will be scientists who understand health care delivery problems. Tomorrow's legislator will understand both science and health care delivery. Was there ever a better example that that of 200 years ago? After all, Thomas Jefferson and Benjamin Franklin were both very capable engineers and legislators.

Health Improvements

I would like to consider how health care can be improved today and forecast the impact, along with other developments, on Americans 200 years from now.

CLINICAL EDUCATION IN GRADE SCHOOL AND HIGH SCHOOL

One of the ways physicians are restricted in their ability to deliver health care is the patients' lack of understanding of their illness. This limitation on the patients' understanding has made it unnecessary for many doctors to advance their knowledge.

As our first step into the future I propose that carefully prepared aspects of clinical medicine be taught in grade school and high school, including the medical and surgical diagnosis and treatment of diseases. Instructors would give a foundation in human anatomy and physiology in order that the students would understand disease dynamics. Candidate diseases are heart attacks, strokes, hypertension, diabetes, lung disease, cancer, and mental disease. At the beginning a few of these diseases would be chosen.

Health education in most school systems now consists of Hygiene I and II and some first aid, with a little controversial sex education thrown in. But new computer-aided education and videotape techniques exist today which make it possible to teach quality clinical education.

In the 1960's, as an aspect of the scientific race with Russia, the "new math" was introduced as early as grade school. The youth who have learned new math and are going on to study engineering and science will benefit from their fast start. Many non-scientists and engineers today understand the use of electronic calculators, communications, or electronics because of having learned some mathematics. Clinical medicine taught in grade school and high school would influence the later life of everyone.

Just as teaching math in high school does not make the student a mathematician or engineer, teaching clinical medicine will not make him a doctor. But at least he will know a good deal more than he does now.

The short-term advantage of teaching clinical medicine in grade school and high school will be better educated doctors and other health professionals. But further into the future our society will become healthier as people in general learn how to prevent heart attacks and ulcers. The hypochondriacal and neurotic segments of Amer-

ica will decrease as people learn more about the diseases that now
are mysteries.

Today, a physician must sit down with the patient and diagnose,
educate, and treat. If unsuccessful at this enormous undertaking, the
doctor is guilty of malpractice. Thus, in the future, when we teach
clinical medicine to our youth, malpractice will be less of a problem.

If this seems to be an unusual proposal, let me give two examples
of how far change can come in ninety years. My great-grandfather,
Dr. Spicer Patrick, a physician who owned a plantation near Charles-
ton, West Virginia, was in every sense a general practitioner. I am
told that he treated Chief Blackhawk with herbs in an area now
called Blackhawk Hollow. Also, back then doctors thought malaria
was caused by vapor from the ground; now every high school student knows it is caused by a special type of mosquito.

Teaching clinical medicine as early as grade school will force us
to organize our knowledge about diagnosis and treatment. For example, Dr. Henry Heimlich of Cincinnati has informed the public
how to diagnose choking on food. He has since proceeded to teach
laymen a specific treatment to save a life by prompt, informed, and
effective action. It is through an understanding of physiology, anatomy, and the dynamics of food choking—and its demonstration on
television—that this training has been made lucid.

Included in the clinical education would be a laboratory course
where the student would learn to take the pulse and blood pressure.
An electrocardiogram would be taken and he would learn its relationship to his heart function. He would compose a computer-
readable summary of his health. This summary, along with others
made later in his life, would have a significant effect on reducing
malpractice problems.

Should the student plan to become a physician, do research in
medicine and engineering, become a nurse, medical technologist, or
emergency medical technician, he could take additional courses in
college.

Sponsored by the Department of Health, Education and Welfare, a physician in Washington, D.C., is trying out ways to teach
older persons how to be their own doctors. That is a good idea, but
why start so late?

It has been estimated that 600,000 Americans die of heart attacks, between 500,000 and 600,000 are afflicted by strokes, and 4000 choke to death annually. The impact of early education to reduce that number should be significant.

Think about what a healthy population we can have 200 years from now! Health problems and surgical procedures will not be such a mystery. And think how advanced the doctors will be. Those just out of medical school will be better educated than those in practice today.

PERSONAL HEALTH RECORD IN COMPUTER MEMORY

As another step into the near future, I propose that each of us have a summary of our health problems, along with prescribed drugs, past hospitalizations, and diagnosis, stored in computer memory for quick reading in emergency situations. (Computer-readable tickets for community transportation are in use even today.) The medical record could be carried on the person or located in a central community data bank, or both, for telephone retrieval. Further into the future this record could be stored in the body itself, perhaps under the skin, for quick computer updating and reading. And it could be stored at multiple locations in the body to protect against accidental amputation.

Treatment now is often delayed in emergencies such as heart attacks because a medical summary is not available to the doctor. He must know immediately if a patient in coma, for example, has a history of epilepsy, diabetes, stroke, prescribed drugs, or surgery. Such a record would not only help the doctor, it would also help to decrease malpractice problems.

Even further into the future blood tests will be taken automatically at the accident scene or in an ambulance. Eventually it will be done without the use of a needle. These tests, along with vital signs and other tests, will be available as computer print-out in the emergency room before the patient arrives. For the patient with chest pain, the probability will be computed by the computer that he is having a heart attack, even while he is at home or in the ambulance.

Vital signs and lab tests for elderly people will be monitored at home, eliminating routine clinic visits and hospital readmissions after heart attacks or strokes. Since telecommunication costs will continue to decrease while transportation cost increases, at-home monitoring will substantially reduce the cost of health care. X-rays or their successors will be taken at the accident scene and reviewed by experts via closed circuit television. And going still further into the future, X-rays taken in space colony hospitals may be sent back to earth for consultation.

ORGANIZATION AND DIRECTION

Why have we always associated advances with wars, and, more recently, space exploration? Are we now to expect advances in health care delivery to come from the national goal to be energy-independent by 1980? Why have we never had a national goal to improve health care delivery? Part of the reason is that in peacetime there has been no organization or direction. And advice to Presidents and Congress is subject to quick change.

The late D. Bronk, President of the National Academy of Sciences for twelve years, said that scientific progress requires determined researchers and teachers of new knowledge who should understand that their progress might be used for power and control of politics.

On the other hand, a panel recently convened by the National Academy of Sciences agreed that higher education is moving in the wrong direction, toward increasing hyper-specialization. So what orderly process helps scientists to know that what they are working on is worthwhile?

One approach in the past was to appoint both lay and scientific advisers to the National Institutes of Health. Many feel these appointments are governed in the final analysis by politics, not scientific considerations. One prime example is that a few years ago Frank Sinatra was appointed to the Heart Council of the National Institute of Health (although it is not clear whether he accepted). Possibly the appointment was made on the scientific merit of his hit record, "You Gotta Have Heart."

How are national goals established? Sometime after the moon landing in 1969, politicians, facing increasing dissatisfaction with the Vietnam war, began to look for a new goal to distract the people and stimulate the American economy. First, in about 1970, Richard Nixon proposed his new goal—to place a man on Mars by 1980. That was not received with much enthusiasm by a stressed public. Somehow we later obtained the goal of conquering cancer by 1980. It, of course, has been argued that this was premature. But after 1969, while we were without a national goal, astrology got a foothold on many Americans; and we are still left with a certain sense of unreality. The energy minicrisis of 1974 gave us another national goal—energy independence by 1980.

Ideally, a national goal should be reachable, affordable, stimulate the economy, and, either directly or indirectly, improve the quality of American life. A possible exception is independent basic research, when it can be afforded.

Sometime in the future billions of dollars could be made available by the government to stimulate development of artificial organs, computerized diagnostic techniques, miniaturized patient monitoring equipment using microcircuitry, the personal computerized medical record, and a program of clinical medicine in grade school and high school. Would this fit an acceptable criteria for a national goal? It might be the first time we ever got improved television sets, home electronic pinball machines, and new military advances through solving health care problems.

America's interest in health care has been increasing. Part of that is a result of America's emergence as a post-industrial society with more interest in services, and there are many opportunities to provide services in health care. I am not sure how much reflects increased intellectualism or interest in preventive medicine.

Computers in Medicine

There are an unlimited number of ways that digital computer storage, retrieval, and computation will advance medicine. Quality of care and efficiency will improve along with a decrease in cost. Tomorrow's physician will be a manager, utilizing information generated by digital computer. The digital computer will read an electrocardiogram with more accuracy, detail, and efficiency than a cardiologist can. With assistance from the digital computer, cardiologists can process electrocardiograms up to five times faster than they can without it. Communication networks allow computer reading of EKG's and consultation otherwise not available to remote community hospitals.

Consider that the public can now buy a hand-held digital calculator having many of the same basic components of a large digital computer for less than $30. This hand-held calculator performs calculations which twenty years ago required a large computer, one big enough to fill a room, costing hundreds of thousands of dollars. Now try to visualize the small size and low cost of a machine which will automatically read an electrocardiogram ten years from 1976. Cardiologists at first will have to help to bring about these changes. But eventually they will have more time to concentrate on numerous other ways to help the patient, including computer evaluation of high risk patients, decisions as to which should have artificial hearts, and general care of the patients.

We have come a long way since 1939, when Harvard instructor Howard Aiken began work on what, in 1944, was to be his Mark I computer, a fifty-foot-long collection of calculating machines.

In the near future the computer will integrate many tests such as electrocardiograms, heart sounds, blood pressure, and X-rays to measure how well the heart is working. *And the computer will not even get to the golf course!*

The computer is making possible the advent of painless tests with very little danger. It will be used to determine patients at risk of heart attacks or stroke and how to prevent them. That will be accomplished by compiling statistics in the computer, using examples of patients who had heart attacks or strokes. Such a compilation does not leave the recall of such statistics to our frail human memories. Our own present work includes teaching the computer to make early diagnoses of heart attacks in the emergency room. This eventually will lead to decreased cost through reducing unnecessary hospitalizations. And we will have a better understanding of drugs for treating heart attacks.

Of course, this is possible because of the dedicated work by doctors of today and yesterday.

One of the computer's claims to fame is its memory: usually it is perfect. A physician's is limited. Thus another use for the digital computer in medicine is consultation whereby certain well-organized facts about diseases and their signs and symptoms are provided to the physician. Tomorrow's physician will be a manager: he will utilize specially programmed computers for consultation to assist in diagnosis. A limitation of the digital computer is that our changing field of knowledge cannot be stored in its memory, thus preventing it from becoming a manager. *Thus, tomorrow's digital computer cannot and will not become a physician.*

For the first time the process through which doctors diagnose and treat is being described by mathematics and systems engineering. This has definitely led to instances where a computer programmed with the techniques can out-perform doctors.

The digital computer is being used to process images generated by X-rays, heat rays, sound waves, electrical waves, and light waves to obtain three-dimensional views of parts inside the body.

Scientists will be looking for new signals to process that will tell them something about what is going on inside the body. Candidates are magnetic fields and special radioactive dyes placed in the body from birth to death.

Over a year ago, the country had the unhappy experience of learning that the wives of the President and Vice President were being treated by controversial surgery for breast cancer. Even as recently as the past month, the medical literature showed the controversy to be no nearer resolution. Through a paper in *Science* a year ago, I proposed an approach by computer that eventually would resolve this controversy. Through the mail I received overwhelming support for the proposal from all over America and other countries. To date, however, our government has done nothing. We have made some theoretical progress on the problem, but without significant funding, progress is slow. This is another example of how progress is made best with continuing minicrises.

Another look into the future: doctors will have available a specially programmed digital computer which, after processing history information and some new non-invasive tests, will indicate the person's risk of having a stroke. A course of action can then be laid out for that person to help prevent an impending stroke. This can be expected to save billions of dollars in care for stroke victims. On the other hand, since certain aspects of the treatment may be surgical, it will require increased availability of specialists to provide necessary treatments until a preventive or cure for arteriosclerosis is found. We thus see why it can be difficult to plan for the next health care crisis. An unexpected diagnostic development could place demand on the health care system that cannot be met. I am impressed with the skills developed by our scientists who work in the area of technology, social, and goal forecasting. They are writing the chapters for the next generation of books on technology and social forecasting. This is done by carefully defining the system. I believe the psychics have learned some of this. They have learned how to use *distant* (i.e. at other geographical locations) *current events,* or *distant past events* to "predict the future." Psychics are the subjective reflection of a new developing science of future management.

It is to be hoped that health planning will not be overlooked in the future.

I have already noted the physician is a manager, while the computer does not have that capability, primarily because it does not have the field of knowledge and judgment the physician does. During the next twenty years we will see computers programmed to do certain well-defined health management tasks. For example, computers will be programmed with alternative ways for you to be treated once you are at a particular health stage. These will at first be relatively narrow management tasks. They may be introduced first in medical school as teaching aids. But after graduation the doctor will find that his less-than-ideal memory will forget these management techniques and he will return to the computer for consultation.

But all this does not take into account a possible breakthrough in duplicating the human brain. When that is accomplished, intelligence can be constructed that has the advantage of both today's digital computers and tomorrow's artificial intelligence. Then computers can become physicians, accountants, mathematicians, etc. Knowledge will advance at rates we cannot comprehend. It has been argued that it is impossible for a human brain to understand its own complexity, but it may be possible to develop such intelligence forms without understanding every detail of their complexity—for example, we still do not know how antibiotics work.

We are trying to understand how the human brain works. We know its memory and intelligence are different from that of the digital computer. The digital computer has the advantage of a perfect memory, both short term and long term. It is far, far superior at calculating sizes or densities than we are. The human brain, on the other hand, has far superior ability at recognizing visual shapes or forms under various translations, rotations, and contortions. I am sure none of you disagree with that.

Even now we can build a hand-held communicator to talk to a computer. A physician could say, "Give Mrs. Smith's 8 a.m. blood work." The computer would "recognize" the physician with 98 per cent accuracy, as long as he restricted himself to a 200-word vocabulary; the computer would reply with the lab result. By the next 200 years people will talk freely with a computer about their medical problems. In fact, you probably will see this before the next twenty years. And the computer certainly will be able to make house calls.

ARTIFICIAL HUMAN ORGANS

We do not usually think of false teeth, glasses, hearing aids, artificial eyelashes, and cosmetics as artificial organs. They *are* artificial organs, however, because they supplement or replace biological living material that may be diseased or unattractive. The electronic pacemaker saves a life by controlling the rhythm of the heart—it supplements or replaces the heart's own biological oscillator.

There are organs which deserve major attention since their malfunction can result in loss of life or major disability. Those organs are the kidneys, heart, lungs, gastrointestinal tract, eyes, and brain—not necessarily in that order. Vision, for instance, although unnecessary for life, is indeed on the major breakthrough list.

Work on the artificial kidney was begun during the German occupation of Holland in 1940. Today, after thirty-five years, a wearable or portable artificial kidney has been developed, although it is not yet practical for routine use. It has been estimated that 18,000 people are now maintained with artificial kidneys in the United States, at a staggering cost to Social Security of $800 million per year.

Today, an artificial heart has kept a calf alive for more than three months—her own heart was removed and replaced by the artificial heart. And, as I have said, each year 600,000 people in the United States die from simple heart attack. Many of them will be saved when a perfected artificial heart is available.

Along the road to achieving implantable artificial hearts and kidneys are numerous spin-offs. For example, the carotid arteries in the neck can now be replaced by artificial arteries when they become clogged, helping to prevent the patient from having a stroke.

We have been working on a lung-assist device which can be worn outside the body. One of the direct spin-offs from space research is solid-state oxygen, which makes possible twenty-four hours' worth of portable oxygen. New sensors are being developed which will allow telemetry of blood gas values from inside the body to a small computer worn on the person. That will regulate the oxygen delivered to a person who has chronic lung disease.

We also are working to adapt the Apollo Double Diaphragm Pump used in the astronaut's space suits as an artificial heart or heart-assist device.

Artificial muscle has been developed and successfully implanted in an animal, replacing its own muscle. This may have application in diseases where muscle is injured or destroyed, as by trauma. It also may have application for attaching artificial limbs.

On the other hand, it has been shown that it is possible to design a paralyzed-muscle stimulator. In many injuries, the victim's muscle begins to die after a nervous system injury. By using a paralyzed-muscle stimulator, it may be possible to keep the victim's muscle from dying and then controlling the muscle for useful limb function. The combined efforts of mechanical engineering and electrical engineering can integrate the artificial muscle, paralyzed-muscle stimulator, artificial nerve, and digital computer for control, to build a new limb. Indeed, that new limb could perform better in certain ways than a real limb does.

An alternative to artificial organs is to grow your own. At birth, cells specific for the body's organs may be removed and frozen. When an organ fails, it may be possible to take the appropriate cell and through genetic engineering grow a new organ. That organ would not be rejected, since it is not foreign, as is an organ from another person. Thus, if we learn to grow organs from cells, then certain artificial organs made by engineers and doctors could become less important.

The artificial limb of the future possesses some interesting possibilities. When we succeed at making artificial nerves, we can have an electronic calculator built in an artificial arm directly operated by your brain. You would not have to use fingers to operate it. The brain would send signals directly down the usual nerves to the artificial nerve, from which signals would operate the calculator. The only thing outside science fiction about this is an artificial nerve which is not rejected by the body. (It is a research area.)

Another important development is the implantable infusion pump for drugs. We all have had the experience of taking pills on a regular basis as prescribed by a physician. Some diseases would benefit from the regular infusion into the body of a drug with the amount of infusion depending on the body's need. Diabetes, for example, is a disease in which there is inadequate supply of insulin, or the regulation of it, normally done by the pancreas, is faulty. An artificial infusion pump is being developed which can supply insulin. A sensor, also implanted, will tell the pump when to supply more insulin.

An artificial infusion pump might supply heparin to reduce the risk of blood clots to the lungs of certain individuals. Possibly one of the most important developments is an artificial infusion pump which would supply the drug Xylocaine when a microcomputer calculated that there was a dangerous heart rhythm. Recall again that 600,000 Americans die each year of a heart attack. Many of those lives might be saved by such a development.

Finally, consider that there may be no blind people 200 years from now. Currently, techniques are being investigated which allow the blind to see through other senses, such as fine touch sensors in the skin. At present, there is a limitation on the quality of a visual image which can be appreciated by a blind person. An alternative approach has successfully involved transmissions of a visual image directly to the seeing part of the brain, again with limited quality. But the invention of implantable artificial nerves could allow direct implantation of an artificial eye.

With all these advances there will not be many handicapped people. In fact, handicaps will be turned into advantages through the availability of modern artificial organs. There will be a more consistent respect for intelligence. Respect for intelligence currently goes through cycles in America: since the moon landing we have been going through a time of decreased interest in intelligence and increased interest in sports and entertainment. We may now be ready for a recycling.

GENETIC ENGINEERING

Genetic engineering is an emerging discipline: it deals with such controversial goals as growing spare human organs or modifying human intelligence. That is one of the developing medical sciences for which we must not be too quick to take a position. There is debate, for example, as to whether scientists have the right to perform certain genetic engineering research. Of course, there also has been debate about abortion, and about death with dignity. Debates in these areas, of course, involve divergent religious beliefs. This reflects difficulty in forecasting due to unforeseen changes in resources, experiences, goals, and emotion.

Within the next 200 years those issues will have been brought up many times. I believe, however, that abortion no longer will be a consideration because of individual planning. Criteria for death and prognosis will be so clear that death with dignity will not be a problem. In any case, new advances will make dignity available.

STATISTICS

There are many diseases for which we do not know the best treatment. Breast cancer and heart attacks are good examples. Of the two, it will be easier to determine best treatments of heart attacks because prospective data is available quickly—the patient's outcome is known within about ten days. As for breast cancer, outcome of treatment is not known for perhaps twenty years. Two hundred years from now, if there still is breast cancer, we will know precisely the probabilities of each treatment outcome for each patient. Do we now study the outcomes of different breast cancer treatments, say to be available in ten or twenty years; or do we assume that there will be no breast cancer because of cancer research? The emphasis today is on preventive diagnostic techniques. I think that we should and will do all three.

Statistics have been largely used for epidemiological studies—for example, the incidence of a particular cancer in Cincinnati versus that in some other city. This does not say much for you or me individually. In the future we could compute probabilities that you or

I will get a particular cancer if we live in Cincinnati. Have you ever considered that matching a person to a certain area of the country or world could improve his health? Perhaps a particular individual would do best on a space colony.

Engineers in the 1960's developed a new area called "pattern recognition." It is not passive, like statistics; rather, it does something —it leads to new devices. An example is a device which can compute the probability a person will have a heart attack or a stroke. It can be implemented by basic digital computer techniques not requiring sophisticated intelligence.

ESP AND ASTROLOGY

Before concluding, I must make a few remarks on the subjects of ESP and astrology. First, let me say that you can expect renewed interest in them whenever America is without leadership or goals. For example, the latest burst of interest began about 1969 and has continued to the present. Some people have a hard time separating the entertainment aspects of ESP and astrology from fact. There may be almost no fact, at present.

On the other hand, recent developments suggest that external influence over the human brain is possible. It has been reported by scientists that low level electromagnetic fields from outside can induce changes in the human brain as reflected by sleep patterns measured by EEG. Also it has been shown that the human brain can emit low level magnetic waves measurable outside the head. There is just too little relevant information to say what will happen in this area during the next 200 years. However, the possibility of modifying human mentation now has a beginning.

PSYCHIATRY

The impact of psychiatry in America probably began with Freud's visit to the United States in 1909. That field continues to evolve. It is now based on concepts of defense mechanisms, personality disorders, neuroses, psychoses, and revolutionary drugs—the major tranquillizers.

About 1960, I participated in some of the early hypnotic experiments being conducted in Boston. Now we have "new" concepts called "biofeedback" and "meditation." I am reminded of a book popular about 1960 called *Sense and Nonsense in Psychology,* and feel that we are now due for a new one in 1976. Many people, for the first time, seem to be discovering their susceptibility to suggestion.

I believe that the power of suggestion is very valuable when properly used. But I would hope that we can achieve a kind of level-headedness whereby we can learn to manage our lives well. It always bothers me a little to see old scientific concepts reintroduced through the media to become only fads.

Perhaps though, that is how part of our education progresses. Each time an old idea is introduced a slightly different way, an inevitable change for the better occurs in America. That may be one of the treasures of our freedom.

With our law of gravity only 400 years old, anesthesia 134 years old, and the first computer 32 years old, we have every reason in America to expect startling breakthroughs in the next 200 years.

Anesthesia was first introduced in 1842, at a time when patients would almost rather die than face surgery. An advanced coronary care unit designed by NASA for a space colony could come at a time when its compactness, efficiency, and low cost would prevent a health minicrisis.

Emerging "third and fourth world" countries with pre-industrial and industrial societies will increase their demand for health care delivery, providing opportunities for the post-industrial societies. Those opportunities will exist especially where computers are involved. For example, satellite communications are already being used to make health care available to remote areas of the world where there are few doctors.

OTHER CONSIDERATIONS

You have heard my views on several aspects of the future of medicine. Just how far and in what directions we progress depends on many additional factors. If we were to have a nuclear war, doctors would be giving increased attention to treating victims of nuclear radiation.

Stepped-up research in how to treat radiation diseases would be required.

Another limited war, such as we had in Southeast Asia, may result in more advanced ways to provide emergency medical services.

If we provide clinical education in high school, as I proposed earlier, our doctors and patients will be better educated. If we do not, a new crisis in health care could develop.

If we have food shortages, doctors will have to give increased attention to diseases caused by malnutrition, many of which now no longer affect Americans.

Once the fragmented facts about the environment are better understood, doctors may have to provide advice on what not to drink or eat, and where.

We could reach a point where drugs and genetic engineering increase the life span to the point where the only limitation is brain aging. Then artificial organs no longer would be a factor.

We may find that diseases, including cancer, can be reduced by widespread adoption of automated controls for dust, smoke, bacteria, noise, odor, and humidity in the home and outside it.

Conclusion

Suppose that in 2176 you could receive cold, total, accurate health care, i.e., diagnosis and treatment with no human error. Imagine a metallic machine, with blinking lights and no feeling, being your savior. You would not be paying one cent for services not rendered. Imagine, at the other extreme, the witch-doctor treatment given to Chief Blackhawk by my grandfather in 1880. Now, in 1976, we are somewhere in between—there is only the beginning of total, accurate, health care, but still a touch of hand-holding and human laying-on of hands.

So as we proceed into the future, who will provide the kindness and sympathy? Should it be a highly trained scientist-doctor? Perhaps it should not be a doctor, but a new member of the health care team whose job it is to understand your problem and talk with you about it. On the other hand, does not that provide a challenge for us to learn to help and love each other, letting science and technology work for us as it should? I am reminded of the saying, written by an unknown author, "I shall pass this way but once, therefore any good that I can do or any kindness that I can show to any human being, let me do it now, for I shall not pass this way again."

IV

JULES
BACKMAN

ECONOMIC GROWTH,

STANDARDS OF

AND

The past decade has witnessed increasing concern over the quality of life. That development represents an emphasis upon social, humanitarian, and ethical considerations and a de-emphasis of economic factors. Nevertheless, most proposals to improve the quality of life do have economic consequences and will affect directly the magnitude of future increases in the rate of economic growth and in the average level of living. In turn, the extent to which quality-of-life objectives can be realized will depend in large measure on the total amount of resources which will be available. Thus, it is important to understand that interrelationship, because change does not take place in a vacuum. The following discussion deals with the economic relationships rather than with the social forces which have been initiating the proposed changes.

LIVING,[1]

QUALITY OF LIFE

ECONOMIC WELL-BEING

Our economic well-being reflects a combination of our standard of living and our quality of life. Our standard of living is measured by the quantity and quality of goods and services available to us. It is this aspect of economic well-being which has received overwhelming emphasis throughout history, as man has struggled first to reach and then to exceed subsistence standards.

The rising expectations throughout the world have been built around hoped-for increases in the standard of living. The goals

[1] The term "standard of living" is often used to describe a goal, but it is popularly used to describe the actual *level* of living. I am using it in the latter sense in this paper.

sought in this area are familiar ones: Do we have an adequate diet? Can we afford steak? Hamburgers? Any meat at all? Do we have decent housing in a good neighborhood? De we have adequate medical care? Can we afford to send our children to college? The answers to these and similar questions give a picture of the standard of living sought and achieved.

Our quality of life, on the other hand, reflects primarily the nature of the environment in which we live and a number of non-monetary aspects of our daily life. Do we have serious water and air pollution? How badly congested is our traffic? To what extent are slums a spreading blight? What kind of care do we provide for the aged? What are the conditions under which we work (e.g. mine and factory safety)? How safe are our streets at night? De we have equality of opportunity in education, housing, and employment?

Unlike standards of living, many aspects of the quality of life are not measurable in terms of their impact upon us individually, and their improvement may affect various groups differently. Everyone, rich and poor alike, gains from a reduction in air and water pollution, and large numbers gain from fewer traffic jams. But only some families gain directly from the elimination of slums. Because the benefits of a better quality of life are diffused and varied among groups, it usually is difficult to obtain a consensus for action. Basically, this is a political rather than an economic problem. The actions taken relate directly to the number of people involved.

More rapid progress is being made in the improvement of the environment than in other areas of the quality of life because to a large extent pollution and its sources can be identified and action can be taken to halt additions.[2] For the same reasons, significant steps have been taken to reduce industrial accidents and to improve safety. But we lag badly in areas such as the elimination of slums, better care for our elderly, safety in the streets, and a reduction in traffic congestion.

Historically, the major aspiration of most families has been to achieve a higher standard of living as measured by the goods and services they could afford to buy. Little or no attention was paid to

[2] It has been reported that the Environmental Protection Agency has promulgated about 2000 pages of regulations applying to states, cities, industries, and individual companies. *The New York Times,* Dec. 2, 1975.

the conditions of the environment.[3] Periodically in the United States there has erupted some public concern over the development of slums in crowded cities or over safety in industry. But many aspects of the quality of life generally were ignored or given little emphasis until the past decade.

Only as our standards of living have exceeded subsistence levels by significant margins has it become possible to develop greater public interest in programs designed to improve the quality of life. Our earlier experience with child labor provides an interesting example: not until the chief breadwinner could achieve a level of earnings at which he could support the family was it possible to proscribe child labor.

The rapid increase in output which has made it possible to achieve higher standards of living has contributed significantly to a deterioration in the quality of life. That situation has been aggravated where population is heavily concentrated in urban areas. Recently, however, public attention has been focused on the pollution problem by a few very significant incidents, such as the oil spill in Santa Barbara in 1969.

Paradoxically, although pollution control may add to total gross national product, the activities which create the pollution never are subtracted from it. That comes about because the equipment required to prevent new pollution or to clean up existing pollution adds to the total output of the economy and thus increases the number of jobs. However, it does not add to the quantity of goods and services available to consumers.

QUALITY OF LIFE: THE UNITED STATES AND ABROAD

Concern over the quality of life is developing only in industrial countries. Most people in the world still live at or below subsistence levels, with barely enough food, clothing, and shelter to survive; thus, the use of scarce resources to improve the quality of life is a luxury they

[3] As far back as A.D. 61, Seneca complained about the smoky air coming out of the chimneys in Rome. In the latter part of the 19th century, concerned groups of citizens protested against the smoke-filled air of London. Bradley R. Schiller, *The Economy* (Englewood Cliffs, N.J.: Prentice-Hall, 1975), p. 633.

cannot afford. For example, throughout South America, Asia, and Africa, per capita incomes generally average $200 a year or lower. At that level of income, the primary concern is survival, not quality of life. One evidence of that problem is found in the fact that life expectancy in those countries is around forty years, in contrast to over seventy years in the United States, and infant mortality rates are very high.

In this country, about 23 million persons are considered to be at or below the poverty level—currently defined at about $5000 a year per family, or $1250 for each member of a four-person family. But note that our definition of poverty is very much higher than the average income in many other parts of the world.

In most industrialized countries, per capita income has moved far above subsistence levels. For example, per capita income in the United States is now about $4200, or more than three times the poverty level. In Europe, the per capita income in 1972 ranged from $939 for Portugal to $4669 for Sweden; the average for all Europe was $2770. Those levels are substantially higher than they were a quarter of a century ago, and in some instances have reached levels where some resources can be diverted painlessly to improving the quality of life. Nevertheless, the differences in per capita incomes among countries are so wide that there are significant differences in the concern over pollution and other quality of life areas.

THE TRADE-OFFS

One criticism directed against programs to improve the quality of life is that the diversion of savings for that purpose will limit the magnitude of future increases in the level of living. This is probably true, but such a development is not new in our experience.

This is the third time in this century that a major trade-off is being made against possible increases in the average standard of living. The first was the demand for more leisure time instead of higher wages, the second was the provision for retirement income in lieu of current consumption, and the third is an improvement in the quality of living at the expense of part of the rise in the standard of living.[4]

[4] A short-term trade-off takes place when income levels permit many persons to go to college and thus postpone their entrance into the labor force until they are 21 to 25 years old.

HIGHER WAGES OR LEISURE TIME?

Around 1900, the average workweek was about sixty hours. As productivity increased, workers were able to command larger incomes even though they worked fewer hours. The desire for increased leisure time was met by foregoing part of the possible increases in weekly earnings. The six- or seven-day sixty-hour week was replaced by the six-day forty-eight-hour week in the 1920's, and then by the five-day thirty-five- to forty-hour week. Despite the reduction in the length of the workweek, real weekly earnings advanced significantly during this period.

After World War II, the amount of leisure time was further increased by the provision for paid holidays, now exceeding ten days in many industries, and by paid vacations which usually range from two to four weeks a year, depending upon the length of service. Those benefits involve costs to companies. If those benefits were not in effect, total output in a year would be somewhat greater and workers' annual incomes could be higher. During this century, the average number of hours worked per year has been reduced from about 3100 to about 1800.

It must be recognized, of course, that part of the increase in output per man hour has reflected the beneficial effects of leisure time,[5] so that the extent to which income has not increased is smaller than suggested by the reduction in working time alone. Nevertheless, some income has been foregone and the rise in levels of living has been lower than it otherwise would have been.

Despite the marked decrease in the number of working hours, the annual real income per capita has increased significantly. Between 1929 and 1974, real personal income per capita increased from $1274 to $3343 (in 1958 dollars). That was an increase of 162 per cent, or 2.2 per cent per year.[6]

[5] This is particularly true when the working day is very long, as the British discovered after Dunkirk in World War II. Shorter hours usually mean less fatigue and hence greater efficiencies and less disruption to production schedules through absenteeism.

[6] Derived from the *Economic Report of the President* (Washington, D.C., Feb. 1975), pp. 268-69. Real weekly wages increased by 144.5% during that same period.

Because of the growing relative importance of federal income taxes, almost one-seventh of the rise in real per capita income was diverted to the federal government to finance its rapidly burgeoning activities.

The record is clear. We have been experiencing both a higher standard of living and more leisure time over the years. In effect, we have opted to use part of the gains in output per man hour to improve our standard of living and part to obtain more leisure time in which to enjoy life.

CURRENT VERSUS FUTURE CONSUMPTION

Another area of trade-off has been the postponement of consumption from one's working life to retirement. With the introduction of Social Security taxes and benefits in the mid 1930's, workers were forced to postpone some consumption until retirement. At the same time, the employer was obligated to pay half of the tax and thus a smaller amount was available to pay higher wages or fringe benefits.

As Social Security taxes have increased, a growing bite has been taken out of current wages. At the start of the program 2 per cent on the first $3000 of annual earnings was paid for by the employee and employer. In 1976, a worker earning up to $15,300 a year paid a tax of 5.85 per cent on his salary and a matching amount was paid by the employer. The combined cost was 11.70 per cent. The result has been a trade-off between present and future consumption.

The magnitude of this trade-off has been further increased for the millions of workers who are covered by company-financed pension plans. To the extent that the money is paid into a pension fund rather than paid out as wages, the worker's current level of living increases less rapidly. The magnitude of the impact cannot be measured solely by the payments into the pension fund since in the absence of such programs the worker might have set aside part of his current income to provide for his old age. However, in light of the great urge to gratify immediate desires, it is improbable that the savings for old age would be equal to the enforced savings paid into the pension funds.

BETTER QUALITY OF LIFE OR HIGHER STANDARD OF LIVING

We are now developing a third major trade-off; a better quality of life in lieu of part of a potential increase in our standard of living.[7] That trade-off is made possible by the enormous productivity of our economy, the result of decades of progress in science and technology, large accumulations of savings, higher quality of the labor force, and improvements in management techniques. As a result, we can now afford to give greater weight to the social and ethical considerations which underlie much of the concern with the quality of life.

Despite its enormous size, however, our economy has limited resources and cannot meet all of the demands made upon it. This is particularly true in connection with demands for the use of savings. Savings are the indispensable prerequisite for investment in plant and equipment, which in turn is the key to economic growth. Shortage of savings is a worldwide phenomenon which is particularly evident in the developing countries and helps to explain why it is so difficult to raise their standards of living.

The programs to improve the quality of life by reducing pollution require a substantial investment. In 1974, for example, the investment by business in equipment to control air and water pollution was estimated at $5.6 billion.[8] That is about 5 per cent of total new plant and equipment expenditures.[9] For some industries, the burden of those investments is relatively high.[10]

The program to limit pollution has acted as a significant restraint upon additions to new capacity. That is particularly true for electric utilities, which are required to make large investments in pollution control equipment at a time when they have had to cut back total planned investment because of lagging earnings and high interest costs.[11] Most of that cutback will mean a much slower rate of

---

[7] Jules Backman (ed.), *Social Responsibility and Accountability* (New York University Press, 1975), pp. 19-20.

[8] *Survey of Current Business*, July 1975, p. 18.

[9] Ibid. p. 15.

[10] See *New York Times*, Dec. 5, 1975, for estimates of costs by chemical, paper, and metal industries executives.

[11] According to a tabulation by National Economic Research Associates, as of Feb. 28, 1975, electric utilities had cut back their construction programs for the 1974 period by $22.3 billion. *Public Utilities Fortnightly*, Mar. 27, 1975, p. 11.

increase in electric power capacity because little of the total reduction is in investment in pollution control equipment. The real price of restraint on expansion in total capacity will be experienced in future years in brownouts and blackouts unless a comparable conservation in the use of electric power is effected. In evaluating the benefits derived from a reduction in pollution, the inconvenience and costs of inadequate capacity must be given consideration.

Resources utilized to improve the quality of life cannot at the same time be used to improve the standard of living. However, that is only one cost. There are others. If the costs of eliminating pollution are too great, it becomes uneconomical to continue to operate a plant and it may have to be closed down. That has already taken place in the cement, paper, chemical, and steel industries.[12] If productive capacity of an industry is reduced or fails to increase because of the pollution control problem, we can experience bottlenecks and shortages, with an accompanying adverse effect upon total economic output and a resulting rise in prices. That that is a real threat was shown by the shortages of cement experienced in 1973 and early 1974.

Although the standard of living will increase more slowly because of such developments, there will also be an improvement in the quality of life, which will provide an offset. On balance, the level of well-being will increase, but the relative mix between the quantity of living and the quality of living will be changed.

Costs versus Benefits

Two broad approaches have been advocated to implement a pollution abatement policy: (1) change market incentives so that they discourage the production that results in pollution, and (2) bypass market incentives with some types of regulatory or legal action. Either approach involves higher costs. How will we pay these higher costs? Higher taxes, if the government finances the bill in whole or in part? Higher prices or lower profits, if the bill must be met by industry? Ultimately, the cost will be borne by consumers and shareholders.[13]

---

[12] Russel W. Peterson, chairman of the White House Council on Environmental Quality, reported that, since 1971, 75 plant closings were partly attributable to environmental regulations. *New York Times*, Dec. 11, 1975.

[13] A poll by the Opinion Research Corporation concerning the cost of elim-

In many cases, the cost is borne directly by the consumer. For example, it is estimated that new government antipollution standards accounted for $284 of the $1010 increase in the price of the Ford Pinto between 1971 and 1975.[14] Higher prices for automobiles have been a factor in the sluggish car sales of recent years. In turn, this has meant a cost in lost jobs. When *all* the benefits and *all* the costs of emission control devices are considered, it is probable that the net gain is smaller than indicated by measurement of decreases in air pollution alone.

The higher cost of low sulphur fuel is borne directly by the consumer when he pays his electric bill, in which the fuel adjustment clause has risen substantially in recent years; the consumer also pays the finance charges for the equipment (e.g. smokestack scrubbers) designed to reduce air pollution.[15] If the cost of cleaning up pollution is borne by government, then it is shifted to all who pay taxes. Regardless of how it is viewed, there is a cost and we must pay it.

Let me emphasize that in calling attention to the costs, I am not saying that we should not take steps to improve our quality of life. Rather, I am underlining the importance of recognizing all of the costs so that we can make rational decisions concerning the speed with which we move and the distance we decide to go in a given time period. The direct and indirect costs and benefits in each of the areas affecting the quality of life must be fully understood if we are to obtain a complete evaluation of the proposed changes and to make intelligent decisions.

---

inating air pollution showed that "Two-thirds said they would consent to paying $250 or more for cars with emission controls that would cut pollution by an additional 10 per cent. Over 60 per cent told the pollsters they would be ready to pay $30 extra annually for electricity to reduce air pollution emanating from power plants. . . . Rather than spend an extra $70 each year for electricity and fuel, 67 per cent said they would prefer adding $300 in additional insulation to their homes. Another 73 per cent said they would choose to turn down their thermostat to 65 degrees." *National Journal* (Nov. 22, 1975), p. 1590.

14 *Business Week,* Jan. 20, 1975, p. 83.

15 The over-all price rise attributable to pollution control has been modest to date. For the year ending March 1974, the Council on Environmental Quality estimated it added 0.5% to the rise in the wholesale price index. Chase Econometric Associates projects an average rise of 0.2% through 1982. See Statement of John A. Busterud (member, Council on Environmental Quality) before Joint Economic Committee, *The Economic Impact of Environmental Regulations,* 93rd Congress, 2nd Session, Washington, D.C., November 1974, p. 136 and Robert Hamrin, "Are Environmental Regulations Hurting the Economy," *Challenge,* May-June 1975, p. 31.

ECONOMIC GROWTH AND THE QUALITY OF LIFE

Our ability to improve the quality of life in the years ahead will be determined to a significant degree by the magnitude of growth in the national economy. It is much easier to meet rising expectations by increasing the total amount of goods and services available—i.e. by increasing the size of the pie—than by redistributing income.

With an enlarged pie, the resources required to improve the quality of life can be obtained out of new increments of output, usually with something left over to raise further the living standards of others. This is more acceptable, politically and economically, than seeking to meet these goals by redistributing the current levels of income, a process which would cause intense opposition from those who would be adversely affected and hence would lead to an increase in social tensions.

The advocates of a no-growth policy believe that we are using up the stock of the world's material resources too rapidly, leaving us with a limited basis for further growth in output which will level off in time—in fact, perhaps, ultimately resulting in a decline in output.[16] That assumption underestimates the possibilities of future technological developments which may add to total resources or make possible the use of marginal resources, as they have done in the past. The development of taconite to supplement dwindling supplies of iron ore provides one recent illustration. Also overlooked is the probability that under the pressure of shortages, a more efficient use of scarce resources will develop. Economies in the use of electric power made in the past two years by many companies provide a current illustration.

Economic growth does not take place automatically, as our experience during the 1930's so well illustrates. At that time there was a widespread belief that our economy had achieved maturity and that further economic growth was not probable. As a result, the prevailing stagnation was reinforced by government policies designed to redistribute income and wealth. World War II destroyed the myth of a mature economy. And as a result, in the post-World War II period

16 See Donella H. Meadows *et al.*, *The Limits To Growth* (New York: Universe Books, 1972).

government policies usually have been designed to encourage growth. A proper economic and political environment is an indispensable pre-requisite for continuing economic growth. Incentives to save and in-vest play a critical role. It is also important that industry should not be entangled in and stifled by the red tape of an expanding federal bureaucracy.

Public policy must be designed to encourage further economic growth, thus minimizing an aggravation of pressing social problems. A redistribution of the income of those in higher brackets would only result in a reduced volume of savings. Since savings play a critical role in facilitating economic growth, the result would be a lower rate of growth, thus intensifying the problem.

Moreover, unless we have a significant rise in total output, there will not be a sufficient number of jobs for our expanding labor force, which increases by one to two million a year. We would face an un-employment problem of monumental proportions or a very sharp reduction in the number of hours worked and probably a decline in the current standard of living. Neither of these alternatives will find ready acceptance.

What is the outlook for economic growth during the last quarter of the twentieth century? First, a caveat. All forecasts involve a spec-trum of facts at one extreme and faith and judgment at the other. The facts usually represent past and current trends. However, there is no assurance that these trends can be projected into the future. Who was wise enough to project the enormous growth in the United States in the past thirty years? The facts available in 1945 portended no such development. Even the optimistic forecasts—few in number—fell short of the realization. And the forecasters had to rely more on faith than on fact in making their judgments.

Who could have foreseen the fabulous growth of West Germany and Japan; the sharp rise and then the decline in the birth rate; the devaluation of the dollar; the enormous growth of computers; the development of miracle drugs, miracle fibers, and the host of other new products; record high interest rates; double-digit peacetime in-flation; landing a man on the moon; and the many other dramatic developments of the past three decades? Clearly, any forecast must be made and received with considerable reservation and skepticism.

Nevertheless I will venture on these uncharted seas. Despite the considerable pessimism concerning the available supply of materials, I am confident that we will have the resources to enable our economy to continue to expand. However, the rate of economic growth probably will be somewhat lower than in the past quarter of a century for at least four reasons: (1) population and the size of the labor force will grow less rapidly, (2) productivity or output per man-hour (OPM) probably will increase at a slower rate, (3) the era of cheap energy is over, and (4) diversion of resources to improve the quality of life must be made. Let me review briefly the factors at work in each of the first three areas; I have discussed the impact of improving the quality of life earlier.

POPULATION TRENDS

The rate of growth in the population is very important, since the total production of goods and services must increase at least as rapidly as the population does if we are to avoid a decrease in the average standard of living. The larger population provides both the demand for goods and the labor force to produce them. Thus, the rate of population increase sets a minimum target for national economic growth.

The median population projection by the United States Bureau of the Census places the total at 262 million in the year 2000, as compared with 212.6 million at the end of 1974. That is an increase of 23.0 per cent.[17] The annual rate of increase would be 0.8 per cent, a much lower rate of increase than in the past quarter of a century, when population rose more rapidly—both absolutely and relatively—from 149.2 million to 212.6 million, or by 42.5 per cent, an annual rate of 1.4 per cent. That large increase in population reflected the baby boom after World War II. However, the number of births has been declining since the mid-1950's, from 4.3 million per year then to about 3.1 million in 1974.

Population projections often have been wide of the mark. During the 1930's, for example, a stable population was anticipated in the early future because of declining birth rates. The big bulge in

[17] U.S. Department of Commerce, Bureau of the Census, *Current Population Reports,* Series P-25, 10, No. 541, Feb. 1975, p. 1.

population after World War II was not foreseen. Then, against a background of the rapid rise in births in this country and the world-wide population explosion, projections of future population growth became highly optimistic—and those forecasts have been punctured in the past decade.[18]

Against this background, the precise forecast for 2000 must be used with reservation. However, there is no indication that we will soon return to the high birth rates of the early post-World War II years. The widespread use of the pill, changing attitudes toward family life (as reflected in the sharply rising divorce rate), and the changing status of women all point to a continuation of lower birth rates. Nevertheless, population will still be a plus factor for economic growth, although a less favorable factor than in the past quarter of a century.

THE LABOR FORCE

The smaller increase in population will be translated into a smaller rate of growth in the labor force. Between 1949 and 1974, the total civilian labor force increased by 30.5 million, or 49.8 per cent; that was an annual rate of 1.6 per cent. If an adjustment is made for the decline in the average workweek from 39.4 hours to 36.6 hours (7.1 per cent) in the same period, the net increase in labor input averaged about 1.3 per cent per year.

It is probable that more than four-fifths of the workers who will be in the labor force in the year 2000 already have been born, so we can project with some confidence what its approximate size will be at that time.

One factor which will hold down increases in the size of the labor force will be the increasing proportion of senior citizens as a percentage of total population in the years ahead. With the widespread adoption of sixty-five as a retirement age, the proportion of older workers in the labor force has been declining and will continue to de-

[18] Herman Kahn and Anthony J. Wiener projected an increase of 27.4 million in U.S. population between 1965 and 1975. By 1975 the total had increased only about 18 million. *The Year 2000* (New York: Macmillan, 1967), p. 168; *Economic Indicators* (Oct. 1975), p. 5.

cline significantly. As a result, many experienced workers will no longer contribute to production, and the burden on the Social Security system will be increased. One effect will be that an increasing proportion of the population must be supported by productive workers whose own standard of living will increase less rapidly. An offset, in whole or in part, can be created by increasing the educational and employment opportunities for minority groups.

The U.S. Bureau of Labor Statistics projects an increase in the total civilian labor force from 91.8 million at the end of 1974 to 121.8 million at the turn of the century, a rise of 32.7 percent. That is an annual rate of 1.1 per cent.[19]

The average number of hours worked per week probably will decline modestly[20] in the years ahead as they have in the past, so that the annual rate of increase in the number of hours worked probably will average less than 1 per cent annually. Although this important component of economic growth will be smaller by at least 0.5 per cent in the next quarter of a century than it was in the past quarter, it should still contribute to economic growth.

THE OUTLOOK FOR PRODUCTIVITY

Gains in output per man-hour (OPM), sometimes called productivity, have contributed significantly to our growth rate in the past (2.3 per cent out of 3.8). There have been many dramatic changes in technology over the years. Nevertheless, as the economy has expanded in size, the *relative* impact of any new breakthrough in technology, no matter how significant, can have only a minor impact on the average annual gain in OPM for the entire economy.

The basic causes of higher OPM are found in advances in technology which lead to a greater amount of plant and equipment capi-

[19] Changes in the entering age for younger people or in the retirement age, or in the proportion of women entering the labor force, could affect these estimates.

[20] The Conference Board has projected a 6% decline in the workweek between 1969 and 1990, or an annual rate of 0.3%. *The U.S. Economy in 1990,* 1972, p. 6. A U.S. Bureau of Labor Statistics study projected a decline of 0.5% per year for agriculture and 0.3% per year for the private non-agricultural sector between 1972 and 1985. Jack Alterman, "The United States Economy in 1985: An Overview of BLS Projections," *Monthly Labor Review* (Dec. 1973), p. 5.

tal available per worker; increasing skills of the labor force, which is closely related to greater educational opportunities; and improvements in management techniques.

Probably the single most important factor is the increase in capital investment. This is why the largest gains in productivity have been in manufacturing, public utilities, agriculture, and mining, where the application of large amounts of machinery and equipment has made possible a sharp increase in the quantity of output per unit of labor. The steam shovel permits a worker to move many times the quantity of dirt that could be moved by cadres of workers using only hand shovels. The computer permits control over complex manufacturing activities that formerly required large numbers of workers. The giant generator produces power much more efficiently than its much smaller predecessors. The Rust cotton picker permits an enormous increase in output per worker as compared with the individual picking cotton.

We continue to expend enormous sums on research and development which will yield important scientific breakthroughs in many areas of our economy. However, technological developments alone are not sufficient. We must also have the resources to finance an expanding productive base and the incentives—the profits—to put those resources to work. Basically, this means that we must have available large amounts of private savings which are not diverted by the need to finance big federal budgetary deficits. In other words, we need prudence both in government spending and in private spending in order to continue to have a rising OPM. Government incentives to encourage capital spending also are important. Without these developments, we will move into the stagnant condition which has characterized the English economy.

However, I am confident that we can avoid the path of England and continue to have greater OPM in the years ahead. In our enormously productive economy, with its millions of businesses, it never is possible to determine where new techniques of management, more efficient uses of labor, or new technological breakthroughs will develop. But I am confident that so long as we maintain what is essentially a free economy, and so long as the incentives to seek new approaches are not shackled, we will continue to experience the changes which contribute to rising OPM. The America of 2000 will differ significantly from what we are today, just as we have changed significantly as compared with what we were a quarter of a century ago.

However, the OPM will probably rise at a somewhat lower rate than in the past for two reasons: the increasing service nature of the economy and the energy problem. In the service industries many activities are on a one-to-one basis. The miracles of modern technology have not been of much help in such service areas as the auto repair shop, the schoolroom, the barber shop, the retail store, and government, although they have played a significant role where the computer can be used.

Historically, the inability to apply large masses of capital has meant a smaller rate of gain and a lower level of output per man-hour for services than in other industries, and as a result the average rate of gain for the entire economy has been held down. As compared with an annual increase of about 3.1 per cent in output per man-hour in the private domestic economy from 1948 to 1969, the increase was 3.0 per cent for manufacturing, 5.7 per cent for agriculture, 5.4 per cent for communications, and 5.9 per cent for electric and gas utilities. In contrast, for services the increase was only 1.1 per cent.[21]

More and more we have become a service-oriented economy. As the relative importance of services increases, they become a dead weight, holding down the average gains in productivity for the entire economy. The full extent of this depressive effect is difficult to measure. However, it will mean some slowing down in the rate of increase in the quantity of goods and services produced per capita and per man-hour.

The Role of Energy

The high growth rate for the economy has been one of the significant factors facilitating rapid gains in output per man-hour. As total volume expands, it is possible to organize the production process more efficiently with the accompanying rise in output per man-hour. Our past growth rate was influenced significantly by an abundant supply

21 John W. Kendrick, "Productivity and Business," *Labor, Technology, and Productivity in the Seventies,* ed. by Jules Backman (New York University Press, 1974), p. 128.

of low-cost energy.[22] However, the era of cheap, plentiful supplies of energy appears to be over. The trend has been evident since the 1950's, but it was brought home to us dramatically by the Arab oil embargo, which started late in 1973, and the accompanying rapid escalation of energy prices.

Unless there are dramatic breakthroughs, we will be forced to economize in the use of energy, and have an accompanying lower rate of increase in economic growth. This would mean a lower rise in output per man-hour and, in turn, in the standard of living. That underlines the importance of making major efforts to improve our technology in the area of energy. With enormous quantities of coal and oil shale and the potentials for solar and nuclear energy, there is a great opportunity for science to effect methods to develop these resources at economical prices to alleviate any future scarcity of energy.

Future Economic Growth

The desirability of maintaining high rates of economic growth has been subject to considerable debate in recent years. Important elements in this debate have included the population explosion, pollution of the environment, the energy crisis, and possible exhaustion of our natural resources. On one side of the debate are the pessimists, who are fearful of the harsh constraints of nature. They are the latest Malthusians; they believe that the end to growth is in sight. Those doomsday prophets emphasize that we will not be able to have much economic growth because supplies of natural resources are being exhausted. On the other side are the optimists, who are skeptical of those prophecies and believe that the limits to growth are not yet on the horizon.

I agree to a large extent with the position of the optimists. However, the net effect of the forces I have described should mean a somewhat slower growth rate than we have had in the past. Even a modest slowdown in the growth rate will be accompanied by many problems—including increased difficulty in providing enough jobs for our expanding labor force; fewer added resources to finance programs to

22 *Economic Report of The President,* Feb. 1974, p. 111.

improve the quality of life; and limited resources to meet expanding demands for greater expenditures by federal, state, and local governments. It is much easier to obtain a consensus for greater government spending when it is financed out of part of the economic growth than when it requires an increase in taxes with the resulting reduction in real standards of living in a stagnant economy.

Nevertheless, it is possible that national output could almost double by the year 2000. Such prospective growth would enable us to increase modestly our present average standards of living, to raise the standard of living for large numbers of underprivileged, and to improve the quality of life. Although such a rate of growth will not be as rapid as in the past nor as large as some hope, it will be grounded upon a relatively high base.

This latter fact often is overlooked when comparisons are made between current growth rates in the United States and in other countries. The level of economic activity and the standard of living are so low in many parts of the world that even large percentage increases yield only minor absolute gains. In contrast, in this country a small percentage increase yields a large absolute gain.

To the extent that we will consent to forego some increases in the average standard of living there will be substantial resources available to improve the quality of life—to reduce pollution, to rebuild our stock of housing, to make medical care more widely available, to improve public transportation, and to make progress in other areas of unfinished business. The developments of recent years indicate that we will move in that direction.

On balance, at the end of this century, our standard of living should be modestly higher and our quality of life significantly improved as compared with the present time.

CONCLUSIONS

We have made a national commitment to improve the quality of life. A basic question is how fast can we move to attain this goal. The energy crisis has slowed down the rate of advance. The trade-off for vital supplies of energy has added a new barrier to the problem in the last two years. Postponement of the date that the goals set for auto emission[23] must be attained is one illustration of what is happening in the new climate. The crisis in municipal finance also will act to slow down local efforts to reduce air and water pollution. Nevertheless, the speed in attaining our environmental objectives is less important than the direction in which we are moving. Even a slower rate of progress should cumulate into dramatic improvements in the environment in the years ahead.

There remains much to be done. Urban sprawl has been accompanied by a significant deterioration in housing, by traffic congestion, by a drug culture, by increasing crime, and by large pockets of poverty. The emphasis upon the nuclear family has left in its wake large numbers of all but forgotten elderly for whom living conditions steadily worsen and for whom nursing care either is nonexistent or is a national scandal. The delivery of medical care is very uneven: many areas of the country are unable to obtain enough doctors and other medical personnel. By trading off part of the possible improvement in the standard of living for a better quality of life we can move to resolve these problems. This will require leadership in all sectors of the economy and at all levels of government. Even more important is the need to face up to these problems on the basis of facts, not politics. With relatively little sacrifice, we have it in our power to improve the quality of life for all Americans in the years ahead. It is time we got on with the job.

[23] However, it has been reported that controls on 1975 models already represented reductions of 60% to 85% in major pollutants. *New York Times*, Dec. 2, 1975.

ROBERT C.
WEAVER

Tomorrow's

I

At a time when the largest city in the nation is on the brink of bank-ruptcy and many others are facing less serious but just as chronic financial binds, it is impossible to ignore the cities' pressing economic problems and the alternatives facing them. As in any crisis situation, there is a tendency, in thinking of the future of the American city, to project current trends uncritically. But economic and social evolution is rarely a straight-line, predictable phenomenon. There are possi-bilities, and historical precedents, suggesting that the current down-ward course of our cities may be arrested. Cities have always been threatened. A few, as, for instance, Pompeii, have been wiped out by natural forces. Others have been destroyed by man. They have always

CITY[1]

been beset by social problems. Their demise has been prophesied time and again, and fiscal crises have come and gone.

Even if cities continue to lose their traditional functions, many of them probably will depend upon secondary ones, such as culture, entertainment, research, education, communication, unique manufacturing, and similar activities. Many major cities in the Northeast and Midwest seem to be moving in that direction. Such adjustments, however, may not solve their problems, for the cities need revenue. With-

1 This is an expanded and annotated version of a Weil Lecture of 1976 under the same title delivered at the Scheuer Chapel in Cincinnati, Ohio on February 8, 1976. Earlier drafts of this paper were read by Ernest Erber, Hilbert Fefferman, Seymour Z. Mann, Henry B. Schechter, Morton J. Schussheim, and Robert C. Wood. Each of them offered comments and suggestions, and the final product benefitted from their contributions. I alone am responsible for the end result.

out it, essential services cannot be provided nor can the quality of urban life be sustained.

Despite the overriding importance of economic considerations in the present and future of cities, those considerations are not all-inclusive. Urban life is complex. Cities, even if economically viable, may be more or less attractive and livable in terms of their safety, the quality of life they provide, and their charm. The latter involves aesthetic attributes, the ability to inspire love in residents and nurture civic pride, and the offering of satisfying cultural experiences.

There are some basic premises undergirding this analysis. The first is that the problems and the potentials of American cities vary. As might be expected, the cities with the greatest economic problems are concentrated in the Northeast and North Central parts of the nation. In those areas urbanization had its earliest and largest incidence. Cities in those regions had significant aggregations of economic activity and unique promise of economic opportunity; they also contained a large, upper middle class of prior residents who had the capacity to move to the suburbs. Less harassed are the newer cities of the Southwest and Western regions. Cities such as Houston, Dallas, and Phoenix are stronger economically than their suburbs are. At the same time, where—as in Minneapolis-St. Paul, Jacksonville, Miami, Indianapolis, and, to a lesser degree, Los Angeles—the entire area has shared certain basic costs with the central city, the economic burdens of the cities have been eased.[2]

The second premise is that federal policy and activity are indispensable ingredients for the survival of urban America in general and cities in particular.

The third is that the state is the only unit of government capable of dealing effectively with certain urban problems.

The fourth is that current tendencies either to assert what Norton E. Long has identified as the concept of "municipal powerlessness"[3] or its corollary, that cities' problems are exclusively the consequence of federal and state action or inaction, are simplistic at best and misleading and inaccurate at worst. Cities are limited as to what they can do to reduce or effectively alleviate poverty, redis-

[2] Austin Scott, "Cities Tackle Timeworn Problems," *Washington Post*, Dec. 8, 1975, p. A-4. (Findings based on a study of the Brookings Institution.)

[3] Norton E. Long, "Another View of Responsible Planning," *Journal of the - American Institute of Planners*, Vol. 41, No. 5 (Sept. 1975), pp. 312-13.

tribute wealth, reduce the level of unemployment, and control inflation. But they can and must contribute toward strengthening their
economic base, softening the process of disinvestment. They can and
must, on their own, lessen the gap between expediture and revenue.
They can improve the quality of life.

The fifth premise is that the American city is the product of our
industrial society, and its decline is, in large part, a reflection of the
continuing evolution and transformation of that society.

The sixth is that America, past and present, has been, and still
is, anti-city.

And the final premise is that race has long been, and remains,
pervasive in shaping American institutions and behavior—and the
current locus of that is in urban America.

My assignment is not to predict the future of the city, but rather
to project what the future portends and hence to point out the moral
dilemmas or moral decisions bound up in the future. Even this restricted objective requires delineation of present conditions, analysis
of how the situation evolved, present and potential roles of the principal participants in the process, and suggestions of possible alternative development of the city. Emphasis will be placed upon the changing role of the American city, recognizing that philosophical and
moral questions are inseparable from the crisis of the city; they are at
the very heart of the crisis and crucial to possible solutions.

II

Movement of the more affluent from concentrations of the poor has
long characterized modern urban life. Jean Gottman, for example,
reminds us that it occurred in the big cities of Europe during the Industrial Revolution.[4] In the United States a similar process has long
been typical, and social standing in American cities has increasingly
been evidenced not only by the type of housing, but the type of neighborhood.[5] Today the latter is the more important. The flight from
deterioration—real or anticipated—has been, in part, a movement

---

[4] Jean Gottman, in Henry J. Schmandt and Warner Bloomberg, Jr. (eds.), *The
Quality of Urban Life* (Urban Affairs Annual Reviews, Vol. 3, 1969), p. 76.
[5] Charles Abrams, *Forbidden Neighbors* (New York: Harper and Brothers,
1955), p. 139.

away from poor immigrants or migrants; it has also, in even larger measures, been a response to the attractions of suburban life.[6]

Ours has long been one of the most mobile populations in the world, and the movement from the center of the city to the periphery and beyond is nothing new. Census data for many years concealed this fact, largely because the city boundaries were distant from the active residential land use. As a result, large-scale building, industrial, and commercial activity could and did take place within the city's limits.

Then several new factors came into play. The first was the revolution in transportation, which facilitated much greater dispersal of the urban population within the city and beyond its corporate limits into suburbs. In the process, economic groups, which had previously not been able to do so, increasingly participated. Other factors were the development of long-distance electric power transmission, which made suburban location of manufacturing feasible, the progressively limited amount of large vacant sites in the city, the restraints on residential development which municipal governments began to effect, and the emphasis upon home ownership, a part of our rural heritage which was subsequently nurtured by federal housing, highway, and tax policies.

Because in recent decades the exodus from the central city to the suburbs peaked at the same time that a large number of newcomers of readily identifiable minorities entered the city, there has been much distortion of what has been involved. Some have confused coincidence with causation. To them desertion of the central cities by middle- and upper-income whites is purely and simply a means of escape from blacks, Puerto Ricans, and Chicanos. Actually, many metropolitan areas with extremely small non-white populations were and are involved in the process of suburbanization. Binghamton, New York; Brockton, Massachusetts; Cedar Rapids, Iowa; Duluth, Minnesota; and Superior, Wisconsin, are just a few examples. Thus color alone cannot account for the great migration to the nation's suburbs.

Had there been no migration of non-whites to urban communities, large-scale expansion of suburbia would still have occurred.

[6] Robert C. Weaver "The Suburbanization of America," paper presented at the U.S. Commission on Civil Rights Consultation, "School Desegregation: The Courts and Suburban Migration," Washington, D.C., Dec. 8, 1975.

And, of course, non-whites participate in the process when they can
do so. As one student of the subject has written: "Without the problem of race Canada's urban history has developed along lines much
like the United States. The homogenization downward of the central
cities with the departure of the affluent followed by the middle class
and elements of the working class is similar."[7]

In this nation, obsession with race has not only distorted popular
understanding of the process of suburbanization; it has also obfus-
cated the true nature of the crisis of our cities. Sternlieb recently
observed:

> *This process of the "defunctioning" of the central city would
> have occurred even if there had not been a problem of race. It would
> have been considerably slower in that case, and the capacity of society
> to adjust to it would have been greater, for the pace of change in our
> central cities has unquestionably been speeded up by racial tensions
> and fears. But serious though that cost has been, perhaps the greatest
> cost of the race factor is that it has obscured the real nature of what
> is going on in the central city. Even if there were no racial difference
> in our society, there would probably still be as many people on wel-
> fare and as many under- or unemployed, and they would still be un-
> welcome among their more affluent fellow citizens.*[8]

The early movement of higher income whites from other whites
who were poor was a class phenomenon. It became racially identified
only after large numbers of blacks moved to the cities. In both instances, the more affluent sought to place distance between themselves
and those whom they considered destructive to their status image and
property values, as well as a threat to their safety. Racial attitudes
translated a class phenomenon into a color problem.

Recent changes in the structure and the social and economic role
of the city have created new and difficult problems for it. In the past
large cities had an advantaged position. Although they then had
much greater expenditure responsibilities than any other class of
government, they also had the greatest concentration of fiscal re-

---

[7] Long, *The Unwalled City* (New York: Basic Books, Inc., 1972), p. 65.

[8] George Sternlieb, "The City as Sandbox," *The Public Interest*, No. 25 (Fall
1971), pp. 20-21.

sources. The latter were generated primarily by forces which increased the property tax base. Included were great concentrations of retail and other economic activities in the central business districts, concentration of manufacturing, and growth of city area (through internal development or annexation), at the same time that the area held a broad spectrum of the population, including the more affluent. "Each of these factors augmented the fiscal advantages of the cities compared to other locations within the state, and within their own metropolitan areas in general, if not to all other places in particular."[9]

Unlike the central city, the basic function and form of which changed only in degree, many of the suburban settlements which have emerged since World War II have little in common with the suburb as it was previous to that time. The contemporary suburb is different from its earlier namesake in both function and form. Without the new functional role it has assumed, today's suburb could not have attained its vast scale. In the process, a new type of human settlement has evolved. It is, in effect, an "outer city" wrapped around the old central city, living in uneasy proximity to the latter, linked through surviving governmental, utility, communications, and banking networks, but relatively independent socially, culturally, and, increasingly so, economically.

Cities' expenditure responsibilities have dramatically increased in recent years as they have received and retained a disproportionate share of very low income people to whom society is now committed to provide special services and transfer payments. Concurrently, the cities have suffered a drastic decline in their relative fiscal resources. Suburbanization has been a principal factor in this phenomenon because it initiated and accelerated the outward movement of the more affluent as well as retail trade, industry, and, ultimately, commercial activities. The older high-tax-producing central business ditsrict increasingly accommodated new functions, such as governmental and other tax-exempt organizations, at the same time that most cities could no longer annex metropolitan economic developments.

The growth and changing role of the suburb not only occasioned the financial bind that most cities suffer, but it also created a divorce

---

[9] Seymour Sacks with Patrick J. Sullivan, "The Large City as Fiscal Artifact," in Gary Gappert and Harold M. Rose (eds.), *The Social Economy of Cities* (Urban Affairs Annual Reviews, Vol. 9, 1975), p. 90.

between the long-term interests of the city and the short-term interests of many who significantly influence its critical problems.[10] Such people no longer have an identification with its future, either abandoning it as a place of residence or disinvesting in its economy.

III

In our governmental structure, the state is the public instrument which can deal directly with regional matters. But the state is more responsive to the affluent suburbs than it is to the city. If the city is to prosper, there needs to be action on the state's part reflecting the fact that the urban complex is an economic and, often, a *de facto* governmental entity, involving both the central city and all its suburbs. That entity will suffer if either element withers.

In matters of urban governmental structure, the state is most important. It, and it alone, can come to grips with intergovernmental issues that are so vital to the urban complex and even more vital to the city. The state also has the capacity to set up machinery for effective area-wide planning and financing, as well as the operation of regional approaches to regional problems, such as waste management, water supply, road maintenance, real property tax administration, productivity in local governments, and the like.

States share with cities and many suburbs limited financial resources. But they also have wide powers. Many of those powers relate to basic issues which harass urban America, involving assumption of functions, establishment of area-wide regulations, and allocation of costs for services and functions that cut across the myriad of local governments. The local governments find legitimacy in state delegation, and the state should act to consolidate them. Most important is the need for states to recognize and react to our urban present. Not only does this require an increased capacity on their part to deal with urban problems but, along with the federal government, they should help guide future urban development.

Because of their wide powers, states can be innovators in social policy and action, and this has often occurred in housing and urban

[10] Long, "The City as Reservation," *The Public Interest*, No. 25 (Fall 1971), pp. 36-37.

development. In the aftermath of the assassination of Martin Luther King, and in response to extreme pressure from Governor Nelson Rockefeller, New York State created the Urban Development Corporation (UDC) in the late 1960's. It had unprecedented powers, including lending authority of some $2 billion; the authority to initiate, finance, construct, and supervise the management of residential, commercial, industrial, and civic facilities; and, most important, the power to overrule local building and zoning ordinances. Utilizing subsidiary corporations, UDC quickly initiated a large volume of residential developments which included moderate and low income accommodations. Since UDC could not subsidize its developments, it utilized federal and state public subsidy programs.

From the start, UDC used its power to override local zoning ordinances sparingly. In 1972, however, it proposed to develop a small amount of low and moderate income housing in the outer suburbs of Westchester County. The reaction to that proposal was so violent that UDC withdrew it, and the following year the legislature rescinded its power to override local building and zoning ordinances.

The Massachusetts Housing Finance Agency (MHFA) was the first to press successfully for a program designed to achieve significant economic mixture in its developments. It, too, can override local zoning provisions which are used to limit or exclude subsidized shelter. MHFA, under the Fair Housing Act it sponsored, requires that 25 per cent of the units in its developments be reserved for lower income households, including those on welfare. The latter housing, as in the UDC program, utilized, primarily, federal subsidies. By June 1974, MHFA had financed 24,114 units; the average mix was 34 per cent low income, 50 per cent moderate income, and 16 per cent full market tenants.

UDC demonstrated that a state agency which not only provided financing but also performed many of the entrepreneurial functions could quickly expand significantly the volume of residential construction, including that for lower income occupants. But by 1974 the Corporation was in deep financial trouble and its future expansion is in doubt. The operation also illustrated that the state faces serious limitations in opening the suburbs to the less affluent. MHFA demonstrated that economically mixed housing is feasible, although it was less successful in modifying racial occupancy patterns.

Both experiences demonstrate the limitations of states in stripping local zoning of its overriding exclusionary impact and facilitating acceptance of subsidized housing in suburbia. That has resulted primarily from the proximity and exposure of state officials to strong local opposition to affirmative action for open and fair housing. Since the states cannot develop sufficient political support to achieve those objectives, they must look to the federal government to do so. Once the latter moves with dedication and efficacy, the states will be an indispensable instrument for feeding into the process regional and metropolitan-wide approaches.

One thing is crystal clear: equitable distribution of responsibility for the urban complexes' social problems and economic costs have seldom been, and cannot be expected to be, achieved by reliance upon voluntary agreements among a multiplicity of local governments. The state must assume an active and effective role, as Minnesota has done.[11] The federal government has the stick which it has not used; the states can and should devise the carrot.

IV

The federal government became involved in aid to the cities not because of its philosophy, but because a vacuum existed. The states, despite their authority, had turned their backs on the cities, and the cities desperately needed financial and other aid. It was then that federal categorical grants proliferated.

But cities perform unique roles. Many of them have long received poor migrants and attempted, successfully for the most part, to aid them in their upward economic, social, and cultural movement. They were able to do this primarily because the total economy was growing. Local governments which perform this function provide a national service and deserve support from the federal government. Involved are sizeable contributions to expenses for basic education, health, welfare, and related activities, at a minimum.

For central cities and many older suburbs, amelioration of poverty is at once a peculiarly vital function and an extremely expensive ac-

11 Dennis Farney, "The Twin City Experiment," *Wall Street Journal*, Mar. 21, 1974, p. 12.

tivity. High incidence of poverty is translated into a declining tax base, decaying neighborhoods, high crime rates, and the flight of the middle class. Although a sizeable, but not the total, incidence of poverty is in the cities, poverty is not an urban phenomenon. It is rather the characteristic of an industrial society that happens to be concentrated within urban centers. Thus, dealing with poverty is a national responsibility. Yet to date we have failed to meet this challenge. The Great Society, at least, made a gesture toward doing so in the OEO, Model Cities, and other programs; subsequent administrations have diluted that effort and failed to provide a substitute.

There are certain other crucial things that the federal government must do. First, it needs to get the economy in order so as to relieve cities (and the entire nation) from the twin ravages of inflation and recession. Substantially high levels of unemployment and low levels of economic activity, paucity of mortgage money, and high interest rates further erode the economic and tax bases of the city. Inflation increases the cost of the services it must provide. These factors, largely external to the city, operated to bring the long-developing fiscal crisis of New York to a head.

Inflation, too, contributes to widening the gap between the incomes of the affluent and the poor, thereby accentuating the impact of poverty in cities. Recession for the nation is *de facto* depression for the disadvantaged. It has extracted a disproportionate toll from the deprived, many of whom contribute so much to the social problems of cities. This is especially true of the aged, the poor, and young people with little or no skills or work experience—elements disproportionately concentrated in cities. The incidence of the resulting deprivation is uniquely severe for blacks, Puerto Ricans, and Mexican-Americans. All the problems which normally harass marginal groups are accentuated when there is a serious slump in the economy. Today the situation has new dimensions. In recent years women and minorities achieved wider and better jobs. With current layoffs, an apparent conflict has developed between the goals of equal employment opportunities and seniority rights, although, of course, both are casualties of economic recession. Too frequently, women and those of non-white minorities, often the most recently hired, are the first fired in a depression, which means that their modest gains of the 1960's have either been lost or are threatened. The depression they experience increasingly takes on the form of sex and race conflict in the labor market at all occupational levels, and that is basically a city phenomenon.

In this period of depression for minorities, the federal government could and should do something effective about its lax administration of laws affecting illegal aliens, which is due largely to inadequate manpower in the Immigration and Naturalization Service. In recent decades the illegal immigrants have been concentrated among Mexicans and those of Caribbean origin. At a time when unemployment among blacks, Puerto Ricans, and Chicanos is at a disastrously high level, such laxity serves, primarily, to accentuate their problems and exacerbate the economic and fiscal difficulties of some of our cities.

There is no way that cities, without federal aid, can either build or rehabilitate an adequate volume of low and moderate income housing, stay housing and neighborhood abandonment, or rehabilitate neighborhoods. The federal effort must not only be viable, but also designed by an administration that wants it to work; it must be sufficiently funded to make a real impact. That is in striking contrast to what now exists.

The main thrust of the Federal effort has been to sweep the realities under the rug. The objective of the 1974 [Housing and] Community Development Act was to get the Government out of the business of building housing and . . . [devise] a way of passing the problem of production back to the private sector. . . . Even if all the problems [of the 1974 Act] were clarified and the climate changed tomorrow, present policy could hardly make a dent in the accelerating need and accumulating shortage that is hitting the poor the hardest and increasing hardship for the middle class. . . . When the Great Society died, so did the objective of 26 million new and rehabilitated homes that were to be achieved by 1978, and so did policy, in the real sense of vision and goals. In its true, national dimensions, housing is one of the most severe and tragic emergencies that this country faces. . . .[12]

As if an inordinate share of the suffering from inflation and recession were not enough, America's ill-housed poor also have to put

[12] Ada Louise Huxtable, "The Housing Crisis," *New York Times,* Nov. 19, 1975, Op. Ed. page.

up with a housing policy that is being administered as if sleepwalkers were at the controls.[13]

More is involved than the specifics outlined above. Unlike most western European industrial democracies, the United States today fails to recognize or act on the fact that only the central government can deal effectively with "natural or social distress that originates over wide areas, crosses state lines and comes to rest on one or more locality."[14]

One such issue is urban land use policy. A program responsive to the current needs of the nation would require a much greater involvement of HUD (rather than a leading role for the Department of the Interior) in the administration of land use legislation. It would offer inducements for opening the suburbs to lower income and minority families, both out of simple justice and because such action would give such people access to greater job opportunities, thereby relieving the cities of some of their social expenditures at the same time that it strengthened the economy of the metropolitan region and the nation. Unfortunately, so far, federal legislation affecting land use planning and control has been directed primarily at resource-use problems. Its basic emphasis is ecological or physical; while social and economic consequences are mentioned, they are not the primary aim.

The impact of the federal government upon the city can be negative as well as positive, as was evidenced a few years ago when its leaders falsely affirmed that the urban crisis was over and proceeded to place a moratorium on those activities aimed to assist in meeting the existing crisis.

It is axiomatic that urban problems are extremely complex, suggesting the need for experimentation and demonstration. Interestingly enough, we, as a people and through the federal government, undertake such rational actions when we make materièl and arms for destroying people and society, but have resisted doing so in order to save people and society. Recent legislation suggests, however, that Congress may be changing its position on the issue. In 1970 it authorized and HUD initiated what soon developed into three types of

13 "Housing Muddle," *New York Times,* Nov. 22, 1975, p. 28.
14 John Herbers, "After New York: The Need for a Federal Help-the-Cities Policy," *New York Times,* Dec. 7, 1975, Sect. 4, p. 7.

housing allowance experiments. That was a major step in the right direction; it, the 1967 OEO experiment to test the effect of income guarantees on work incentives, and a few other activities suggest that we may be approaching a new level of sophistication in these matters.[15] If so, the cities will certainly benefit. It is interesting to note in passing that single-function, categorical programs seem best adapted to demonstration and evaluation.[16]

The rise of revenue sharing was a direct consequence of the proliferation of hundreds of categorical grant programs and a disenchantment with growing detailed federal review. (I discount the rhetoric about turning the government back to the people.) An early move in that direction was the block grant approach in the Model Cities program; it came to full bloom with enactment of general revenue sharing and provision of special revenue sharing in the Housing and Community Development Act of 1974. As might be expected, we have moved from the extreme of too great federal regulation to not enough. And that is to the detriment of the future of American cities.

Many mayors and some state officials, conscious of social problems and wanting to do more about them, are under unrelenting pressures to spread available resources among many neighborhoods and groups. "If the mayors are to give special attention to the poor out of proportion to their political strength, they need special justification."[17] Previously, the system of federal categorical grants protected well-motivated mayors from the resentment and anger of middle class voters who felt they were left out or neglected.

There is increasing sentiment among students of the problem to the effect that three types of federal aid to cities—general revenue sharing, special revenue sharing, and categorical grants—are needed.[18]

---

15 Of course, there are complicated problems peculiar to experimentation in social matters. See Alice Rivlin, *Systematic Thinking for Social Action*, Brookings Institution, 1971. And there are equally complex legal and ethical problems. See Rivlin and P. Michael Timpane (eds.), *Ethical and Legal Issues of Social Experimentation*. Brookings Institution, 1975.

16 Bernard J. Frieden and Marshall Kaplan, *The Politics of Neglect: Urban Aid from Model Cities to Revenue Sharing* (Cambridge: MIT Press, 1975), p. 255.

17 Ibid. p. 248. This point was made earlier; see Morton J. Schussheim, *The Modest Commitment to Cities* (Lexington, Mass.: D.C. Heath, 1974), pp. 142-43, 202ff.

18 Dennis A. Rondinelli, "Revenue Sharing and American Cities: Analysis of the Federal Experiment in Local Assistance," *Journal of the Institute of Planners*, Sept. 1975, pp. 319-33; and Frieden and Kaplan, *op. cit.*, p. 249.

Community development revenue sharing, as enacted [in the 1974 Housing and Community Development Act] is a big improvement over the categorical programs it replaces, but neither the law itself nor HUD's first administrative regulations reflect some of the key lessons of model cities and other programs of the 1960's. The performance criteria calling on local governments to focus their programs on eliminating slum conditions and meeting the needs of low-income residents are weak and ambiguous. . . .[19]

One of the greatest threats to the future of the American city is the attitude of hopelessness and helplessness concerning public programs designed to deal with social and urban problems which was cultivated by the Nixon administration. That was nurtured by attacks upon "throwing money" at such problems, at the same time that the administration was pressing for general revenue sharing, which may well prove to be the most glaring example of such an approach. A less subtle expression of the current wave of hopelessness is found in the assertions that the Nixon administration inherited unworkable programs, while ignoring or attempting to conceal its own administrative ineptitudes. Jesse Burkhead has noted that the rationale for the moratorium on grant-aid programs was that they had not worked, although many had hardly been given an adequate trial. He identified fiscal considerations as the determining factor in their cessation.[20]

Oakley Hunter, chairman of the board and president of the Federal National Mortgage Association, identified five obstacles to housing production. Two of them he characterized as being relatively recent:

. . . The Federal Housing Administration and some other HUD units charged with delivering housing services to the American people have passed through periods of reorganization, controversy, disuse and changes in mission which have left them weakened, as HUD itself has recognized.

Finally, we are in a period when clouds of doubt and discourage-

[19] Ibid. pp. 250-51; see also note 13, above.
[20] Jesse Burkhead, *The Political Economy of Urban America: National Urban Policy Revisited,* Gappert and Rose (eds.), *op. cit.,* pp. 60-61. See also William E. Farrell, "Unsolved Problems of Housing and the Poor," *New York Times,* Dec. 13, 1975, p. 56.

ment have obscured for many of the organizations and individuals
concerned with housing those rays of hope that are essential if they
are to find their way to consensus that makes fruitful action possible.[21]

There is a major federal role that cannot be expressed in terms
of dollars and cents. It is a matter of philosophy and national leadership. Involved are not only aid in developing, championing, and
funding programs, but also understanding and articulation of changing values in contemporary society. Such participation and analysis
coupled with sustained and effective financial aid and an inspired
vision of the potentialities of urban life would serve to bring our
people together in support of a meaningful effort to make American
cities economically viable and attractive. This type of leadership was
offered the American people within the memory of some who may
read this paper. During the New Deal, Franklin D. Roosevelt demonstrated that the nation could be inspired to restore hope.

There needs to be vision as well as commitment. There must be
knowledge as well as action. And we look to national leadership to
supply this. Without such a Federal posture cities cannot prosper in
America.

V

Cities can do many things for themselves. Perhaps the most significant thing they can do is to restructure and reform their public
schools. With the movement of manufacturing to the suburbs, a larger and larger proportion of jobs in the city has become white-collar,
administrative service, and professional. Most such jobs require, at the
minimum, a meaningful high school education. Lack of programs to
accomplish this has created a real urban mismatch, involving the
educational requirements of the remaining good jobs in the city and
the educational qualifications of many of those still residing within
its boundaries.[22] Over the short run, the impact of better schooling

21 Oakley Hunter, *A Housing Policy for Today* (Washington, D.C.: Federal
National Mortgage Association, 1975), p. 4. (Remarks delivered before the National
Association of Housing and Redevelopment Officials, Los Angeles, Calif., Oct. 14,
1975).
22 Long, *op. cit.*, pp. 27-29.

would be slight, both because time would be required to upgrade the schools and because such action cannot create jobs. But in the context of the future of the city, such action has real potential and significance.

One of the most frequently cited impetus to flight from the city is the high incidence of crime. A large part—in many categories a sizeable majority—of the perpetrators are young. According to a recent report of the Federal Bureau of Investigation, children between the age of ten and seventeen, who comprise 16 per cent of the population, account for almost half of all arrests for violent crime and theft.[23] And there is impressive correlation between high rates of unemployment and crime, especially among young people. Wider employment opportunities, requiring, too, higher levels of jobs, would surely upgrade the security of the city.

Having a larger supply of literate and functional high school graduates would result in several benefits. First, it would provide greater choices to such graduates—depending, of course, that jobs are to be had. More could opt for a job rather than having to pursue higher education if they hope to find anything more than joblessness or low-paid, dead-end employment. Most of them have no such choice today. In addition, the smaller number electing to go to college would be exposed to a much lower rate of attrition, thereby also reducing the fiscal burden on the taxpayer while rendering it less difficult to preserve standards.

Delivery of services is, of course, a vital element in the quality of urban life, and greater productivity is a factor of this. Most public functions are highly labor intensive. Improvement in productivity will be, at best, a long-term effort; but that does not mean that it should not be initiated or that it cannot make a contribution to the survival of the city. Productivity depends upon the quality of management as well as the effort of the worker. In contemporary America, productivity also requires management which will articulate that jobs are important and that workers are performing vital and significant functions.

The potential for upgrading productivity through management reforms is suggested by a recent experience in New York City, where,

23 Marcia Chambers, "Radical Changes Urged in Dealing with Youth Crime," *New York Times,* Nov. 30, 1975, p. 58.

despite the layoff of almost 1500 sanitation workers and reduction in the frequency of garbage collections, city streets and sidewalks were reportedly as clean as they had been before the reduction in personnel. Although the initial consequence of the cut in manpower was a precipitous drop in cleanliness, within a few months the lost ground had been recovered. That took place after the mayor ordered the department to raise productivity and provide better supervision. He also replaced the Sanitation Commissioner. While the survey was not able to draw definitive conclusions as to the causal factors in the recovery, it did demonstrate that higher productivity is a possibility in city services.[24]

By March 1976, however, the situation had again deteriorated. Personnel reductions had claimed almost 2000, and the number of trucks out of service because of mechanical defects had increased from an average of 600 to 700 on any given day. Morale was low, and the new Sanitation Commissioner was pessimistic about the department's ability to deal with the expanded volume of refuse expected to be occasioned by the Bicentennial activities, the Democratic National Convention, and the accumulation of trash from warm weather clean-up projects at the time when there will be the highest incidence of vacations among sanitation personnel.[25] These recent developments indicate the impact of seasonal peak loads, worker morale, and maintenance of equipment upon productivity in this type of municipal service.

In many cities, personnel policies and procedures, civil service regulations, and middle management are in need of review and reform. It is within the city's power to do much of what is required. Then, too, as cities have to tighten their belts, they will need to question the utility of many functions which seem to be justified more by longevity than usefulness.

In this era of increasing power of municipal labor unions, successful efforts to improve productivity and reduce costs of services must involve these unions. Recent events in New York City suggest that unions which in the past were said to be indifferent to cost (al-

24 Ari L. Goldman, "Study Finds City as Clean as in '74 Despite Layoffs," *New York Times,* Nov. 30, 1975, p. 1.
25 Nathaniel Sheppard, Jr., "City Trash Pick-ups 'at a Critical Stage,' Officials Assert," *New York Times,* Mar. 7, 1976, p. 22.

though often acutely attuned to the importance of productivity) can be induced to take a different posture when they are involved in a concerted effort to ward off disaster for the city and themselves. What we now know suggests that some municipal unions would have responded to an effort to obtain productivity increases in exchange for gains at the bargaining table. Few efforts were taken in that direction in the late 1960's and early 1970's.

Cities need to reappraise their potential for attracting and holding certain types of manufacturing and other businesses. Comparative costs and efficiency are, of course, basic, and not unrelated to the efficiency of local government. There are two other elements which are even more controllable by the city. The first is the nature and magnitude of municipal taxes. If they continue to proliferate and increase, those businesses which are mobile will continue to leave the city. Similarly, the city is in a position to take more positive action in the form of reduction of unnecessary reports and associated costly regulations, especially for small businesses. But more important, each city needs to evaluate its attributes in terms of managerial talent, labor force—existing and potential—location, and the like in order to identify possible lines of business activity which could contribute to the revival of the city in terms of jobs, revenue, and tax receipts. Such action takes on real significance in light of the probability that high rates of unemployment may continue to harass cities even after economic recovery gets under way.

Cities, in their quest for viable functions and economic base and in identifying possible roles and specialties, must do so in terms of the present and future rather than the past. This is complicated by the fact that cities have varied in their capacity to annex territory, have differing locational advantages, compete in differing degrees with activities elsewhere in the urban complex, and have other peculiar attributes. There is no universal pattern for their success.

As suggested above, economic viability alone cannot and will not determine the future of the city. Its natural resources, in terms of location, topography, and vistas, its climate, its charm, both physical and in terms of its population, its possibilities for privacy and anonymity for the more sophisticated, and the access to, and the quality of, services and facilities it provides are equally important. I have devised a simplified formula for evaluating the attraction of a city; it is the degree that residents and visitors walk in its streets. A basic element in this, obviously, is the level of safety that it affords.

In dealing with productivity and delivery of services, cities face a complication in that the services provided by public agencies are of less interest to many than the jobs and invoices that are generated by the process. That occasions a conflict between job seekers, potential bidders on goods and services, and aspirants for political power, on the one hand, and consumers and taxpayers, who look for quality of services at lower cost, on the other. Although such conflict is a universal phenomenon at all levels of government, it is accentuated at the local level, where public officials are so closely and intimately involved in the process.

One of the most pressing and difficult problems the city faces is to articulate the trade-offs between an increase in jobs in the private sector and a possible reduction in social services. Consideration of that issue is significant not only because of its intrinsic importance, but also because it is symbolic of the difficult problems which face city-elected officials.

Proponents of high priority for private enterprise employment make these points:

The cities have been losing private sector jobs for over a decade and the slack has been made up partially by expenditure for social services, which, in turn, raises taxes and accelerates the loss of private employment.

That further erodes the economic base of the city, reducing the revenues it enjoys and increasing its expenditures.

The poor, who, as all Americans, look to be a part of the mainstream of the nation, really want to enter into the established private work sector.

Those assertions are in the tradition of classical economics. Within that context, they are valid, and, certainly from the point of view of the city's fiscal crisis, they are sound. But priorities incident to budget cutbacks are not exclusively economic considerations; for many of those affected, they are not long-run issues, and the assumptions of classical economics are refuted by the peculiar problems and experiences of the disadvantaged. Then too, as John Maynard Keynes observed over a generation ago, in the long run we will all be dead.

If—and the *if* is important—an increase in private enterprise jobs would be assuredly translated into significantly more employment for the poor, the proposal would have greater appeal to them. Unfortunately it is not assured; for despite recent improvements, private industry, by and large, is uncomfortable with other than middle class white collar workers, especially if they are identifiable minorities.

The urban poor are asked to give up some of their current social benefits for future, more rewarding and fulfilling employment. But they are far from convinced. They do not see evidence that employment will grow in the immediate future. Then too, proponents of cutbacks in social services are also advocates of stressing control of inflation at the cost of high levels of (private) unemployment. Despite recent modifications in the situation, they are still the symbol of minorities' traditional exclusion from private employment. The poor are suspicious of Greeks bearing gifts.

In the context of cities' current problems, it is possible that dedicated leaders and cooperative principals could deal effectively with the issue. The first requirement is a realistic analysis of the matter, similar to the one outlined above or more sophisticated. If one accepts my diagnosis, a possible approach would involve the following:

A reform of the educational system, as outlined above.

A commitment from private industry in the city to increase the employment of qualified resident youth from ethnic groups that have long been either excluded or given low priority in such employment-- a commitment which will be difficult to achieve unless the national economy is revitalized.

A commitment from those same groups to institute and maintain on job training to facilitate upgrading.

An agreement that cutback in basic social services will go in tandem with employment of a larger number of city residents.

Responsible government's establishment of machinery to carry out the program.

Not only must city government commit itself to a workable trade-off in this matter, but it must also articulate its position effectively. That will not be easy, for despite crisis responses to the problems of the disadvantaged, city government is usually more responsive to the middle class. The matter of private employment versus social services affects all elements in the city; it needs to be interpreted in terms of the future viability of the community. A decade ago socially oriented, federal categorical grants eased the situation. Today the city is more on its own, both politically and financially, as "the philosophy behind revenue sharing . . . shifted the burden of dealing with large concentrations of poverty to city governments, which generally choose to use the money for basic, rather than social services."[26] The city cannot escape the resulting hard decisions, and it will not be able to make rational ones unless it places the problem in a proper perspective and effectively explains its program.

VI

As one ventures to speak of the future of American cities, one must first attempt to envision the potential role of the city in the United States in future decades. If such a projection is to be realistic, certain facts have to be recognized. One thing is certain: we cannot and will not revert to the past. Economic forces and changing values dictate a new role for the city. In the changing environment of recent decades, it should be obvious that the central city no longer has a non-competitive function as the exclusive economic and cultural center of the metropolitan area. Technology, in transportation and communications in particular, has eroded that situation, although central cities still retain significant advantages of centrality.

[26] John Herbers, *loc. cit.*

If the future of American cities is projected on the basis of current trends (a procedure I earlier questioned), the outlook is bleak. Most of our cities have experienced loss of population; disinvestment is the rule and private investment the exception.[27] It is doubtful that most American cities will grow physically, demographically, or economically, and that implies economic decline, which will result in reduced tax revenue. Reduced revenue inspires advocacy of cutback planning to deal with the situation.[28]

In an article dramatically entitled "The City as Sandbox," Sternlieb has envisioned the city's major problem as lack of economic value. The city lost its *raison d'être* with the cessation of great waves of migration to it and the termination of a great need in the nation or in the city for unskilled labor. In this milieu, cities as we have known them are simply irrecoverable. The sandbox envisioned is a place that is sustained by money from elsewhere (primarily the federal government), used to support a huge bureaucracy, which, in turn, is sustained "by the plight of the poor, the threat of the poor, the misery of the poor, but which yields little in the way of loaves and fishes to the poor." Such efforts, however, have in his opinion, symbolic importance, indicating to the urban poor that something is being done for them. Sternlieb does not despair completely, however, for he suggests that we could reject the sandbox and design policies "to insure that everyone has an opportunity for . . . [productive] work, even if this involves cost to over-all economic growth and wealth."[29] Of course, such a cost is not inevitable and depends, in large measure, upon national policy and leadership.

Long is somewhat less pessimistic, but far from reassuring. Thus, while he believes the cities can find new specializations to justify their existence, he recognizes the difficulties of doing so. In such uncertainty, the city can become a reservation. Long sees revenue sharing as "payment by the outside society to the city's bureaucracies and politicians to maintain a poor farm and a reservation. . . . [B]usiness and the productively employed, seeking escape from tax burdens,

[27] Norman Krumholz, Janice M. Cogger, and John H. Linner, "The Cleveland Policy Planning Report," *Journal of the American Institute of Planners* (Sept. 1975), 298.

[28] Herbert J. Gans, "Planning for Declining and Poor Cities," *Journal of the American Institute of Planners, op. cit.,* pp. 306-7.

[29] *Sternlieb, op. cit.,* pp. 15, 16, 18, 21.

poor services, and crime, migrate or suburbanize. Even the keepers suburbanize. Black teachers and policemen follow white to the suburbs."[30]

Long presents an alternative. In involves self-help and development of a local economy co-equal with that of the outside society. That would call for a mixture of more effective education and neighborhood organization.[31] What Long seems to deemphasize is the role of the federal government and other outside elements in the process.

In a recent analysis of the prospects for the inner city Ernest Erber has concluded that it will survive for this historical epoch, but with vastly changed functions and, perhaps, form. He believes that it will continue to exploit the advantages of centrality in a limited number of activities, but they will often be captive. It will retain labor-intensive, but low-productivity, low-earning, manufacturing industries by virtue of a low-wage labor force that is sustained by public assistance and transfer payments. Erber, too, envisions the city as an urban reservation for the poor.[32]

He is not without hope. Mass infusion of money into central cities could buy time, and if these resources were well used, it could reverse the extreme dichotomy between inner and outer cities.

But such reduction of extreme differences between inner and outer populations involves . . . a leveling down of peaks and a leveling up of valleys on the metropolitan area's social terrain. This assumes wisdom and farsightedness on the part of the advantaged that has been rare in the history of human affairs.[33]

The costs of stagnation and the possibility of the city as a sandbox or a reservation are not only economic decline. They also involve grave social costs and potentially frightening further erosion of the quality of city life. That is not without deep roots in our society.

. . . By default we have concentrated "outsiders"—poor, black and volatile—at the vulnerable centers of our metropolitan complexes;

[30] Long, "The City As Reservation," pp. 32-33.
[31] Long, "Another View of Responsible Planning," pp. 314-15.
[32] Ernest Erber, "The Inner City in the Post-Industrial Era," Declan Kennedy and Margrit I. Kennedy (eds.), *The Inner City* (London: Paul Elek, 1976), p. 39.
[33] Ibid. p. 43.

besides them we have concentrated others, "semi-outsiders," poor, white and volatile. We have given over the function of policing to still others, barely insiders, who have bitter memories of racial competition and conflict. We have built self-perpetuating enclaves of people who are indifferent to, if not enemies of, the dominant moral order of middle-class white society, and they can be moved against the physical structure of that society.[34]

VII

We in this nation came late to our urban destiny. Although we have been in the midst of an urban revolution for at least a century, and a predominantly urban nation for more than fifty years, we have had difficulty in adjusting to those realities. The national ideology—the philosophy of frontier and farm—was one reason for this. It led us to cultivate suspicion of city life. Our political system enhanced this problem. Conscious that the nation was dominated by rural constituencies, political leaders had long ignored or failed to understand the mounting problems of the cities, and many still do, as recent events in Washington during New York City's travail have demonstrated.

Two major problems have developed—one in the central city, the other in the suburbs. Simultaneously, they have harassed the urban complex. That in the core city implies a moral and social failure; that of the suburb implies a political failure and a moral vacuum.

The American city has traditionally provided a way station for the waves of immigrants who came from abroad, and by and large it has treated them well. Though the newcomers were not strangers to hardship, they learned the language and new skills and many of them went up the long tenement trail to relative affluence and acceptance into American society. But in recent decades the historic role of the city has deteriorated badly. Its humanizing influence has faltered, and the urban poor are increasingly insulated from the larger society. Millions of black and other minority group families are trapped in racial ghettos, and once trapped, they are hard put to break away.

[34] Scott Greer, *The Urban View* (New York: Oxford University Press, 1972), p. 336.

There is no one reason. Inferior housing and inferior education go hand in hand, and together they foster and reinforce inferior employment opportunities and inferior incomes. They are parts of a cycle of intertwined causes and effects, strengthening each other like the strands of a rope which binds and chokes millions of American families. Opportunity and the traditional urban choices have not been generally available to these recent newcomers. Nor does the economy need a labor reserve of unskilled workers. With prosperity all around them and a television set in the tenement room, these facts are not lost on those trapped in the ghetto. It is neither a Negro problem nor a city problem: it is a national problem. The United States faces today, as it has always faced, a choice between devoting the understanding, resources, and commitment necessary to deal effectively with this issue or risk the social costs of harboring a sizeable alienated element without a vested interest in the society. For many this is a moral issue; for a much larger number it is a matter of survival.

In the suburb the operative words are proliferation, scatteration, and fragmentation. There has been a proliferation of governments into tiny suburban enclaves and special districts. They are piled one upon another in endless procession. That creates a scatteration of political entities, rivaled only by the frequent wasteful scatteration in land use patterns. There is often more history than logic in the location of local governmental boundaries; and special districts often overlap and compete for the same resources. The *de facto* single urban complex is governed by a multitude of operationally independent governments. They are in reality interdependent, but because of their fragmentation, common problems cannot readily be solved for the common good. On the other hand, urban America is basically a unit which encompasses the central city and its surroundings. There are many problems which cross existing political lines and cry out for area-wide treatment. But such treatment collides with our dedication to localism of mind and institutions.

Progress in meeting urban problems requires commitment and belief in society's capacity to achieve results. There has always been a lag between what man is capable of doing and what he elects to do. Inspired leadership is required to close this gap. For unless the American people believe that they can have a workable, attractive, and meaningful urban society, they will never achieve it. At the same time, there is always the danger that in the effort to raise the vision and expectations of the populace more will be promised than can be delivered. Too great dependence upon public action *per se* will lead to a fool's paradise of expectations and ease of achievement; unreasonable and unsupported repudiation of it damns us to unjustified hopelessness.

The very timing and function of American cities were inimical to their orderly development or aesthetic appeal. Our cities are not replicas of sixteenth-, seventeenth-, or even eighteenth-century cities, which were frequently projections of the personality of a ruling prince, dynasty, a church leader, or perhaps a commercial oligarchy. By the end of the Industrial Revolution, all that had changed—particularly in the Anglo-Saxon world—for the city then became primarily both the *instrument* and the *result* of industrial development. Economic efficiency was the primary goal. This is not to say our cities were without positive attributes. But there was a lack of over-all design, too little concern for beauty, and too great emphasis upon material facilities—qualities which were universally prevalent in industrial nations of the era.

American capitalism had a rational, matter-of-fact, pragmatic justification which emphasized work and function. It was concerned with order. In the small-town mercantile and artisan way of life, work and thrift were immediately rewarded. As the economy expanded, the facts of life—and the abuses of capitalism—eroded those values and exposed the system to attack.

Lincoln Steffens and Jacob Riis graphically delineated the harsh realities of urban life in the nation. Later writers, such as Mencken, Sherwood Anderson, and Sinclair Lewis, challenged existing values. That challenge was supported and substantiated by institutional developments—the rise of large cities and suburbia, the concern for conspicuous consumption (so expertly identified by Veblin), and the acceptance by the *nouveau riche* of status as the mark of success. The old idea of delayed gratification in a world of scarcity was replaced for many by a glorification of plenty and high consumption, often motivated by advertisements. Such changes were subsequently accentuated by the revolt of black Americans, the disaffection of youth, and the new role of women—and all of those people found conventional values less and less meaningful, especially with the rise of a national culture via the movies, radio, and television. The value system was weakened, and, for some, undermined, by attitudes and behavior which deviated from the basis of the system.

In all those ways the moral justifications of authority have been eroded. The economic system seemed to be without a unified value of its own. Actually, the older values had been questioned by many long before the revolt of youth, the eruption of the ghettos, or the push for women's rights. To the troubled on the extreme right and to many lower middle class working people, the questioning of conventional values was devastating. The new ideology and values seemed to be the ranting of radicals and intellectuals, and a repudiation of established morality. The commitment of many Americans to hard work, authority, and self-reliance appeared to be challenged. And indeed it is by many current patterns of behavior.[35]

Thus the nation, as well as the city and the rest of urban America, is faced with a basic choice. Do we attempt to restore the order, rigidity, and moral surveillance of yesterday? Or do we risk the challenge to order and stability?

Those who oppose the changed values—and they are many—often see their origins in the city. They would either advocate its decline or expose it to "benign neglect." But we cannot ignore or forget our cities. The people living in them will not let us; even if they would, we should not. Cities were not put in certain spots by accident. They are often in locations which, for the most part, would be picked for human habitation and certain economic activities if we started *de novo* to site them. The location may be a beautiful spot overlooking a waterfall; it may be a natural harbor; it may be at a central point where man has created the crossing of a series of highways and railroads or where nature has engineered the convergence of several rivers. Many are physically attractive places in which people ought to live. And the important job is not to do away with existing urban centers and replace them with new ones at another location; it is to rehabilitate and make them viable while we create the new.

[35] The above four paragraphs are an expansion of an analysis first developed in a paper delivered Mar. 6, 1973; see Weaver, "Can Problems of Urban America be Solved?" *The Urban Challenge* (Washington, D.C.: General Accounting Office, 1973), pp. 1-16 (mimeographed).

There is a fundamental choice: do our cities meet the needs of their people or do they cut their cloth according to their current financial resources? For some this is an economic question. Others articulate the moral issue incident to living beyond one's means. In the final analysis, this poses the question of whether or not there will be greater state and federal financial assistance to cities. Earlier I have indicated that many cities do not have revenue sufficient to meet the basic needs of their people, *even if they achieve fiscal reform and administrative excellence.* To ignore that fact is to determine that the most disadvantaged and deprived of the urban population are to become even more deprived. The financial sins of many cities obfuscate the issue, in that they are reprehensible and cry out for reform, but for large part cities are well-motivated from the humane point of view. There was, for example, prayer and hope that the federal government would bail New York City out of its deficits.

Is America prepared to say that substantial federal aid is to be withheld from cities which have both the greatest concentration of the needy and declining revenue? Or will national leaders have the fortitude and capacity to convince the voting majority to provide assistance commensurate with needs which are concentrated in the central cities and increasingly located in cities of many older suburbs? There are those who welcome the demise of the city, resent it for both its moral and financial sins, or believe it deserves to suffer. They have no problem. They are for local fiscal responsibility and letting the chips fall where they may. On the other hand there are those who believe that we can and should ameliorate the ravages of poverty; they advocate greater and better targeted federal financial assistance to the city. More than federal dollars are involved. What they and local funds buy in terms of services depends primarily upon the nation's ability to control inflation (which competent authorities assert will alone add almost twice as much annually to the HEW budget as the entire department spent two decades ago[36]), the quality and efficacy of the involved programs, and the productivity and efficiency of municipal governments.

If central cities are to prosper, they have to establish priorities. That involves planning at the local, regional, state, and federal levels.

[36] Jonathan Spivak, "Putting a Lid on Social Programs," *Wall Street Journal,* (Dec. 31, 1975), p. 6.

But there are many who see planning as the essence of communism or socialism and oppose it as morally and economically wrong, as well as ineffectual. Society has to decide if it is to involve itself in a planning process, or repudiate such planning as inconsistent with its values.

Excessively high zoning and development standards coupled with building regulations, especially in smaller urban communities and involving minimum lot size or housing costs, are the most effective instruments for maintaining homogeneity and residential exclusion in suburbia. In recent years a new instrument has been devised to accomplish these and associated objectives. It is the so-called "anti-growth" and "no growth" movement.

Anti-growth and no growth policies, the impact of which are concentrated in suburbia, take various forms. In some instances, localities place vacant land into holding zones, thus enabling them to permit rezoning for development (and developers) they approve. Or localities announce a temporary suspension of rezoning, subdivision approvals, or issuance of building permits. Other devices have been developed to fix the ultimate population of a community. A resolution to accomplish that was passed by the voters of Boca Raton, Florida, in 1972. More sophisticated approaches are distortions of development timing, allegedly based upon availability of adequate infrastructure. Perhaps the best known is the Ramapo, New York, ordinance which defers development of housing for as long as eighteen years on a large part of the vacant land controlled by the town.

The most pernicious devices (in part because they are so plausible in light of past ecological neglect and abuses) justify limited growth or no growth policies on the basis of ecological considerations. Often that conceals the fiscal reasons, generally involving avoidance of capital expenditures for schools, water, sewers, and associated facilities which sooner or later would be paid for, at least in part, by current residents.[37]

The fear of uncontrolled growth—a dramatic repudiation of the nation's long commitment to expansion, largely on the basis that it would increase tax rolls and spread per capita costs at the local level—is gaining support. Suburban communities pressed by inflation are listening to arguments about the hidden costs of growth. Less fre-

[37] Herbert M. Franklin, "Slow-Growth and the Law," *Housing Development Reporter*, Vol. I, No. 4 (June 1973), p. B-1-6.

quently, if ever articulated, is their long-time aversion and opposition to the entrance of lower income and minority households.

How do we recognize ecological interests and still permit necessary urban growth and housing, while facing up to associated social and economic needs of the disadvantaged? Already defenders of suburban exclusion are wrapping themselves in the popular bunting of concern for the environment. Championship of excessive standards for clean air, clean water, and associated environmental attributes can and will stymie urban development and inhibit the free movement of excluded groups. And it gives respectability to moratoriums on building permits, density limitations, establishment of population maximums, and associated local actions.

The ecological crusade can, and probably will, drive up housing costs, laying the heaviest burden on the poor. Production of housing at the right price and near the source of employment may adversely affect the environment in some instances. Inevitably, there will be a conflict between adequate urban growth, socially oriented housing, democratic patterns of shelter, provision of sufficient energy, and economic expansion on the one hand, and all-out ecology on the other.

Currently, federal approaches to economic residential dispersal and urban land use policy are as much if not more a matter of executive action than legislative intent or statute. Because, increasingly, there is a conflict between what the Congress enacts into law and what the Executive carries out, the courts are engaged in adjudication of disputes. Litigation designed to require implementation of provisions of the Housing and Community Development Act of 1974 has been sponsored by the General Accounting Office, citizens' organizations, developers, and individuals. The most recent court case was related to residential exclusion and land use policy.

In order to understand what is involved, it is necessary to refer to pertinent provisions of the 1974 Act. Among the primary objectives of the Community Development title of the Act were:

Expansion and improvement of the quantity and quality of community services, principally for persons of low and moderate income.

More rational utilization of land.

Reduction of the isolation of economic groups within communities and geographic areas through spatial deconcentration of housing opportunities for lower income persons.

A unique feature of the Act was the Housing Assistance Plan (HAP) required from each locality desiring a community development block grant. Among other things, HAP is supposed to promote the dispersal of housing for low and moderate income households within metropolitan areas. Each plan is also supposed to give an assessment of the housing needs of lower income persons "residing or expected to reside" in the community. There was, however, little evidence that these objectives were being achieved. This had been due to several circumstances: the requirements of the law remained an unrealized promise,[38] and there was no effective program to provide lower income housing throughout the urban complex.

As it now stands, the Act will have minimal impact upon effecting more rational land use on the area-wide level. That follows from the fact that Housing Assistance plans and applications for community development grants are structured on a local rather than an area-wide scale.[39]

Recent litigation affecting seven affluent suburban communities surrounding Hartford, Connecticut, is significant. In that instance, a Federal District Court judge enjoined HUD from granting community development funds to localities which failed to make projections of how many lower income residents they expected to move into their borders, despite the legal requirements for so doing.[40]

The decision punctured the widely held fantasy that there are in this country homogeneous, problem-free communities that do not have to share the burdens of poverty and economic inequity prevailing elsewhere in the society. It is dangerous enough for the nation's future for a sizeable segment of the people to be so mistaken, but it

[38] *The Housing Assistance Plan: A Non-Working Program for Community Improvement?* (Washington, D.C.: The Potomac Institute, Inc., 1975).

[39] Weaver, "Commentary" on Charles J. Orlebeke, "A Framework for Housing Policy," Harvey S. Perloff (ed.), *Agenda for the New Urban Era* (Chicago: American Society of Planning Officials, 1975), p. 160.

[40] Lawrence Fellows, "Hartford Blocks Aid for Suburbs," *New York Times*, Jan. 29, 1976, pp. 1, 66.

is worse for the Administration to encourage such myopia by disregarding the law.[41]

By January 15, 1976, HUD had revised its regulations relative to submission of Housing Assistance plans. While the revisions increased the specificity of the requirements for estimating the volume of households expected to reside in a community, they still left much to be desired. There was no requirement for applicant communities "to indicate a program of action or a strategy for realizing the goals that they are now required to articulate in the HAP. It makes little sense to require communities to adopt policy plans specifying quantitative goals for the provision of housing but not requiring them to specify the strategy to achieve such goals."[42]

Effective implementation of the 1974 Act, which mandates more rational land use and deconcentration of housing opportunities for lower income households, is a current legal issue and will remain so, at least in the immediate future. Its moral implications are more enduring.

VIII

The incidence of tax-exempt properties in urban America has grown dramatically in recent years. That sector in New York City now represents 40 per cent of the whole, as against 28 per cent two decades ago. In Boston the figure is about 53 per cent; in Washington it is 49 per cent. Suburban cities are not immune; in Rye, New York, exempt property has increased from 10 to 33 per cent in the last thirty-six years, and that is typical of much of Westchester County.[43] Most of those tax-exempt uses are authorized by state law and the affected localities have no options. Because religious, charitable, educational, and a multitude of non-profit groups are involved, it is extremely difficult, and in some instances politically impossible, to effect fundamental changes or reforms.

[41] "The Hartford Lesson," *New York Times*, Jan. 31, 1976, p. 24.
[42] The Potomac Institute, Inc., *Memorandum 76-1-2*, Jan. 28, 1976, p. 5.
[43] Carter B. Horsley, "Spread of Tax-Exempt Property is Accelerating in City," *New York Times*, Dec. 21, 1975, Section 8, pp. 1, 3.

Urban communities face the dilemma of bowing to current political reality or starting now to seek a more rational and financially sound approach. Its leaders must recognize, however, that the latter course of action, desirable and just though it may be, can be futile and is sure to arouse intense and arbitrary opposition. Good economics is not always good politics.

In common with states, cities and other urban governments face difficult and complex choices relative to civil service. The system, initiated as an antidote to political patronage, is now under heavy attack, and in the name of good government. Chicago, Minnesota, and Oregon have abolished their civil service systems. About a hundred other governments are overhauling theirs.

Some assert that local civil service is hopelessly archaic and inflexible, that it flies in the face of modern management techniques. Minority groups oppose the system, and courts have frequently upheld them, ordering one hundred localities to scrap their utilization of civil service regulations in hiring and promotion of police and firemen on the grounds that the tests involved were racially discriminatory and unrelated to subsequent job performance. Civil service has been weakened, too, by the rise of municipal employee unions.[44] Yet there are many who still view civil service as the bulwark against political patronage. In my own experience, during 1933-44 and in most of the 1960's, I have seen the federal civil service system function effectively under inspired and capable leadership.

The issue is charged with the vested interests of those protected by civil service and haunted by their and others' memories of abuses prior to its initiation; at the same time, civil service poses an impediment to efficiency and productivity in local governments. It presents a dilemma of major proportions.

Another troublesome situation exists in the controversy over whether spatial dispersion of non-whites or significant upgrading and rehabilitation of the ghetto is preferable. Actually, there is no real dilemma: we must move simultaneously in both directions.

A sophisticated approach recognizes the intrinsic locational value of many black ghettos, urging that blacks control, occupy, and develop them, using organizational and entrepreneurial talents in the

44 Jonathan R. Laing, "Civil Service Setup, Born as Reform Idea, Now Hit by Reformers," *Wall Street Journal*, Dec. 22, 1975, pp. 1, 13.

process. But this position does not imply that all blacks are to remain in the central city. Some who articulate it recognize the economic and psychological costs of exclusion from the suburbs, where new housing and new jobs are concentrated. They would agree with Congressman Parren J. Mitchell, who said, while speaking before the Thirty-third Annual Conference of the National Association of Housing and Redevelopment Officials in 1971, "Let's get the record straight. I'm not at all sure that most blacks want integration. . . . I am sure that we want equal access to the housing market. . . ."[45]

Busing to achieve integration in public schools is a more immediate and pressing issue. Senator George McGovern has characterized it as one way to pay the bill for the *ancien régime* of racism; Senator Joseph Biden has said that it is a bankrupt concept. For others, the issue is more complex.[46]

School desegregation and integration have displaced housing as the most controversial area of race relations in urban America—perhaps because, in large part, both issues' incidence is more immediate. Advocacy of busing for school integration has the potential for occasioning rapid realization. But it provides little opportunity for supportive rhetoric and delayed actuality, as does support of open occupancy in housing. As a result, housing integration has suddenly acquired a host of new advocates who propose it as an alternative to school busing for integration. Of course, both busing and integration in housing have important roles, but instant advocacy of the latter and repudiation of the former present a moral issue.

Some positive developments could result from the plight of New York. In its metropolitan area, there are evidences of greater understanding of the need to spread the burden of supporting municipal services beyond city limits:

> *If nothing else, the crisis has shown that New York's economic infection can't be contained within the borders of its five boroughs; the city's credit crisis has had grave budgetary and fiscal consequences for every level of government in the region [and beyond the state].*

[45] Weaver, "Housing and Associated Problems of Minorities," Marion Clawson (ed.), *Modernizing Urban Land Policy* (Baltimore: Johns Hopkins Press, 1973), p. 61.

[46] Diane Ravitch, "Busing: The Solution That Has Failed To Solve," *New York Times*, Dec. 21, 1975, Sect. 4, p. 3.

But even as a sense of shared urgency dawns on New York's neigh-
bors, resistance to regional cost-sharing is stiffening. One thing is
clear: If the state and suburbs pitch in to bear more of the responsi-
bility of city government, they will do so only out of an instinct for
self-preservation.[47]

There are, of course, serious impediments to regional approaches
to problems which, while concentrated in the city, have area-wide
implications. A major one is the attitude of the middle class toward
the poor, involving the ever present elements of class and color, as
well as associated moral issues. During the early rise of urbanism,
annexation was attractive because it brought city services to outlying
populations, while at the same time central cities expanded their
economic and real estate tax bases. Today it is associated with sharing
the costs of providing social and other services for the disadvantaged,
often raising the issues of economic and ethnic population mix and
of political dominance. Affluent suburban whites frequently oppose
it as an instrument to introduce poor and black participation in what
they consider their preserves. Most blacks see it as a means of preserving or restoring white political control in the central city at the
same time that they themselves have or are developing the muscle to
achieve control.

In any event, the nation cannot avoid a reexamination of the
desirability of metropolitan government reform as a state function;
nor can the federal government remain aloof. The type and form of
revenue sharing can either encourage current proliferation of local
governments, as is now the case, or it can become a positive factor in
encouraging area-wide approaches to area-wide problems.

IX

The preceding analysis, while recognizing the city's deficiencies and
the crucial role of the states, emphasizes that the impact of national
forces has been paramount in determining the pattern and problems
of urban America. Three developments have been basic: the long-

---

[47] Barry Newman, "Suburban Dilemma: New York's Neighbors, Hurt by Fiscal Crisis, Agonize Over Aid Role," *Wall Street Journal*, Dec. 29, 1975, p. 1.

standing national ideology that fosters anti-city sentiment; the equally long-standing heritage of racism; and the recent tendency to despair that public action can deal with social and urban problems, often expressed by the mistaken notion that in a complex industrial society the least government is the best government. Other events have had significant influence, including:

Regional shifts of population, first from rural to urban areas and most recently from the industrialized North toward the South and West.

Changes in the scale and functioning of metropolitan areas.

Movement of population and economic activities out of central cities, resulting in their inability to meet expenditure requirements out of available revenues.

Rise of economic and racial exclusion in suburbia.

Proliferation of local governments.

Current recession and inflation.

One major consequence of these developments, primarily external to cities, is the probability that many of the cities will decline in size. The psychological impact will be accentuated because of our long commitment to the virtue of expansion and identification of it as an indispensable condition for urban health. But it is possible for central cities (and urban areas) to adjust to smaller size. Regardless of increases, decreases, or stability of population, the income mix is more significant than sheer numbers. Of course, cities which lose population face painful adjustments; however, decline in size *per se* need not be catastrophic. Abandonment of neighborhoods and housing, which is a symbol of the physical and economic decline of central cities, can, for example, become a setting in which densities and housing costs are reduced, open space increased, and more productive land uses devised.

More basic are the fiscal problems which will result from population changes. In the process, the immediate question is not whether there will be a cutback in expenditures, but whose consumption should be cut. Are interest payments on bonds—guaranteed by state constitutions, by city charters, and by law—paramount over labor contracts negotiated through collective bargaining? Will determination of such issues be based on legal requirements, contract provisions, ability to make sacrifices, or through negotiated trade-offs? If the latter route is chosen, what of groups and individuals that have little bargaining power?

The answers to those questions raise fundamental philosophical issues, involving, among other things, the future role of the city and possible trade-offs between strengthening its economic base versus provision of vital services. They pose, too, perplexing moral dilemmas and involve difficult moral decisions.

In a future in which the growth of population and the comparative level of economic activity may decline, energy is of uncertain availability and increasingly costly, and resources are becoming relatively scarce, the streamlining of central cities and the strengthening of decentralized urban regions seem desirable. What is needed is a federal policy to give direction, understanding, and assistance to smooth the transition, as well as to upgrade the capacities of state and local governments to cope with the new situation. At the same time, federal and state policies, programs, and assistance alone will not be effective unless cities upgrade appreciably their administrative efficacy and fiscal management. External levels of government can provide greater resources; the cities will have responsibility for the deployment and utilization of the resources available to them.

There is a danger that since the incidence of many of the nation's ills is concentrated in the central city, the nation may assume that they are exclusively city problems. Because difficulties are more devastating in one location does not mean that they are created wholly or primarily by their locus. Thus, the incidence of problems in central cities does not make them city problems alone. Rather they are rooted in the values, culture, economy, and institutions of the United States. By the same token, the future of the nation's cities depends primarily upon the country's attitude toward them. Will the current trend toward assigning low priorities to cities continue? Or, in the complexities which face us as a nation, will we recognize that unless cities are preserved and the problems of the urban complex recognized, the nation as a whole will decline? For it is in urban America that many of our most pressing problems must be solved.

Felix G. Rohatyn, chairman of the New York Municipal Assistance Corporation (MAC), places the issue in a long-time perspective:

A Federal "Marshall Plan" for the reconstruction of our older cities would be both stimulative and, by providing both employment and production, anti-inflationary. Although politically unpopular at present it is morally right. Shouldn't we rebuild our cities and employ our poor rather than spend billions on nuclear overkill? Why were Cologne, Frankfurt and Milan more entitled to Federal support than Indianapolis, Baltimore and New York?[48]

The central city and its many unique and subtle resources are worth saving. Within its borders are enormous wealth, infrastructure, and human talent, as well as a multitude of cultural institutions. It affords a way of life which appeals to many, although not a majority, of our people. In this period of concern for conservation and avoidance of unnecessary duplication of infrastructure, there is strong rationale for its preservation.

While survival of the city will require much more enlightened federal urban policy and programs, it also calls for abandonment of the doctrine of municipal helplessness. Such an attitude breeds paralyzing avoidance of self-analysis and provides an excuse for not facing up to the city's own defects and responsibilities. At the same time it postpones realization by the citizenry that they must tighten their collective belts and effect major reforms and economics in municipal government.

There is a wide spectrum of possibilities for tomorrow's city, ranging all the way from revival or relative stability; to a holding action; to decline, sandbox, or reservation status; or to gradual extinction. For most American cities, the era of rapid growth seems to be past; that does not necessarily mean, however, that rapid decline or possible extinction is inevitable. Nor does the possibility of relative stability or modified revival imply that either will be achieved.

[48] Felix G. Rohatyn, "A 'Turning Point' for the City," *New York Times*, Feb. 6, 1976, p. 29.

Man has created urban America. He can change it to meet his needs and aspirations. This is why, despite the travail of recent years, I am hopeful about the future of the city and urban America. For many centuries urban residents have been a hardy breed, taking pride in overcoming problems. The future of the city and urban America depends upon the continuation and strengthening of this attitude, and with a more realistic and sophisticated understanding of the complexities involved. Pragmatism, long a national characteristic, will be important, too. When the chips are down, most Americans, if given inspired leadership, will, I believe, recognize the waste of human, cultural, and natural resources in the city's demise.

The viable American city I envision will not be replica of the city-state, the medieval towns of Europe, or the small towns and cities of yesteryear. Nor will it be the post-World War II city. It will seek to capture some of their qualities, modifying economic and social abuses of yesteryear's urban America, while refusing to destroy the economic and technical advances that have been made. It must be intolerant of poverty amidst plenty and insistent upon a new emphasis on ethical values and aesthetic matters. It will look inward to identify and correct its deficiencies of administration and finance while, rightfully, expecting state and federal assistance that is justified by the heavy burdens imposed on it from outside. The city of the future must always remember that people are its most important asset. It must also recognize that racism is evidence of moral decay.

VI

MARTIN E.
MARTY

THE AMERICAN

TRADITION

Whenever an essayist or lecturer defines and defends the terms in his
title, we can expect him to say something like this: "Every word in
my title gets me into trouble except, of course, the definite article."
In the present case, however, the definite article may be the occasion
for the greatest trouble. How can one speak of *the* American tradition? Before we make any attempt at finding coherences which will
make sense, it is necessary that we be reminded of the incoherences
of American society and its many subcultures.

An illustration of those incoherences might come from the index
section of any book that tries to deal in broad terms with America.
Doing so almost gives one license to agree with Emmett Grogan that
"anything anybody can say about America is true."[1] No outlines of an

1 Quoted in Art Spiegelman and Bob Schneider, *Whole Grains* (New York:
Douglas Links, 1973), p. 52.

AND THE

AMERICAN

TOMORROW

American plot or tradition seem at first glance to emerge. Take a book with an appropriate title for our circumstances, *Coming Apart,* which is "an informal history of America in the 1960's" written by William L. O'Neill.[2]

Within the index of that book one may choose a section. The "Ma" portion (which includes "Mc") will serve well. William F. Buckley once sent a copy of his own new book to novelist Norman Mailer, an old foe of his. Buckley wrote his little greeting next to Mailer's name in the index section, knowing that there Mailer would immediately get the message. Buckley assumed that authors have giant egos and great curiosity, and that Mailer would look for his own name before he would read the book. I myself, no stranger to

2 William L. O'Neill, *Coming Apart* (New York: Quadrangle, 1971).

the "Ma" sections, feel at home there in a search for *the* American tradition.

What sense shall we make of the following conglomeration? There in the index are Eugene McCarthy and Robert McNamara, on opposite sides of the sundering Vietnamese War. Joseph McCarthy is remembered near Mao Tse-tung, a non-American who helped divide America. Malcolm X is there, but so is Lester Maddox, at the other end of the racial pole. Marshall McLuhan, who told us, in effect, that in the media world whatever was, was right, is listed near Herbert Marcuse, who said the opposite. *Machismo* shares space with the Mattachine Society, a homosexual organization. Norman Mailer, of course, is there, but so is the Maharishi Mehesh Yogi. Marist College and Charles Manson, Jayne Mansfield and Abraham Maslow, "Masscult" and maxi-skirts, the *Making of a Counter Culture* and MAAG (American Military Mission), John L. McClellan and Floyd McKissick, George McGovern and Mad Dogs, Manufacturing and Marijuana—all helped make up the 1960's. Those names represent only half of the entries under a one letter-combination of one-seventieth of one index of one book from one year from one corner of one library. Is there a *the* American tradition?

A second problem in the title is the word *American*, which seems to be at the same time too small and too large an entity for attention. Too small—in our global village or on our spaceship earth it seems provincial, even chauvinist, to isolate something so small as one nation for a discussion of values. George M. Cohan, the Broadway showman who knew how to use patriotism, reminded us that "many a bum show has been saved by the flag." Should we not speak of the human family, the race itself, the human tradition? But "American" is also too large a category. Most of the citizens of this nation draw their main inspiration from their subcommunities, subcultures, religions, tribes, racial and ethnic groups, movements and causes. Tribal deities often have more potency than does the God of the nation. Why use the national experience, a middle-range term, for those purposes?

Nor can we easily slide past the term *tradition* in a society usually seen as producing what Crèvecoeur called "this new man, the American." We are told that ours is a culture that constantly consumes or forgets its past, steel-balls its historic buildings, neglects its archives, produces "Now" people, and blurs the very concept of tradition. For how many people is a living tradition a source of values at all?

Hidden behind the three words of the title is another assumption. My contribution to this collection of essays is to concentrate on religion. Why does that word not appear in the title? Dare one equate "religious" with "traditional," or see religion to be integral to tradition? Let me begin by defending the assumption that the two have much to do with each other, an assumption based on a theme of Paul Tillich which argues that religion is the soul of culture and culture the form of religion. One would not think of interpreting cultures that derive from Buddhist, Islamic, Hindu, or similar influences without some awareness of their religious grounding. Every visitor to American shores who wishes to make sense of life in this nation also finds it important to reexplore the religious roots of this culture, as many natives do not. While we cannot write "religion equals tradition," we can see that the deepest sanctions for the tradition are religious.

By traditional, I refer in part to what Ortega y Gasset called the *creencias* and *vigencias* of a people. *Creencias* are the ideas that we are, and not merely those we hold. They are the small pool of constitutive beliefs that are so deep they seem to be part of us. *Vigencias,* on the other hand, are the binding customs of the culture, the habits and manners, the ethos and style that become characteristic of wide elements in it. Countercultures know very well what they have to counter when they face those beliefs and ways. Beliefs and customs come to us from history, from the past. Hannah Arendt, with William Faulkner, believed that

"The past is never dead, it is not even past," and this for the simple reason that the world we live in at any moment is the world of the past; it consists of the monuments and the relics of what has been done by men for better or worse; its facts are always what has become (as the Latin origin of the word: fieri-factum est suggests). In other words, it is quite true that the past haunts us; it is the past's function to haunt us who are present and wish to live in the world as it really is, that is, has become what it is now.[3]

[3] *New York Review of Books,* June 26, 1975.

That past is mediated through that partly artificial entity called the nation, which provides at least one kind of grasp on universal reality. Our task now will be to try to discern not some outlines of "religion in America," but "American religion." Whoever addresses such an issue inevitably selects and produces a construction of reality. No two people will come out with exactly the same outline, for they deal with elusive realities. One feels almost like the daring and reckless child in a story of encounter with her mother:

> Mother: *"What are you doing, daughter?"*
> Daughter: *"I am drawing a picture of God."*
> Mother: *"Don't be silly, darling. No one knows what God looks like."*
> Daughter: *"They soon will."*

No one knows what the American (religious) tradition looks like. But, in a sense, they soon will.

One cautionary word: there is no claim here that the five elements to which I shall point are unique to America. They are distinctive. They are sufficiently widely shared in America and not sufficiently widely shared by other nations or peoples who are apart from or who preceded the American precedent to warrant some measure of identification.

I. PLURALISM

Pluralism is the obvious fact about America, and it is certainly distinctive. With the spread of technology, mobility, and mass media, an increasing pluralism is known all over the world today, in many nations. America is not the first country to include more than one religious grouping, to be sure. But nowhere before or elsewhere has there been variety on the scale experienced here, or such a widespread acceptance of the grounding of that diversity, or such celebration of its positive values. No foreign visitor fails to observe it. In a sense, to say that our tradition is pluralistic seems to say that America has no tradition: how can the "many" be a "one"? Yet Americans have dealt with their "many" in a way that has caused a kind of "one" to emerge.

On the fact of the variety one need not long dwell. *The Year-book of American and Canadian Churches* annually lists between 220 and 230 widely recognized church bodies. Some Roman Catholic authors who want to perpetuate an old tradition that finds Protestantism to be false because it is both diverse and divided provide longer lists. Israeli scholars, who have to keep tabs on every millennial or apocalyptic sect in America because so many of them have their eye on Israel's role in the plot of history's end time, can list hundreds more. And those listings refer only to more or less formal groups. They do not even begin to reach out to the attitudes of private citizens, or to the ephemeral clusters, cells, movements, and impulses that can be discerned in the index to *Coming Apart*.

What is further distinctive about American pluralism in the religious tradition, beyond its sheer quantity and scope, is the fact that it has generated an assumption: "Any number can play." Most pluralisms have been based on the idea that there should be a host culture and then there can be guest cultures. First there is an official, legal establishment, and then dissenters are allowed to exist in the society on some terms or other. Assent is present so that there can also be dissent; conformity is present so that there can be nonconformity. Parity is another question entirely. The United States, of course, learned its new plot very slowly. It took a couple of centuries before a true legal basis was provided, and down even into the middle of the twentieth century it was still hard for privileged religious groups to learn that in mores and ethos they had to yield privilege and share equal space and time with groups they had once considered to be marginal.

In Holland there existed a pattern called *Verzuiling*, a columnization based on completely separate Protestant-Catholic-Jewish institutions and idea-structures. In many nations there were spatially divided territories in which one religion would be present with a monopoly, while at some distance another had to be reckoned with in its territory. But America became a crazy quilt of overlapping religious groups. The believers invented denominations in order to house their separate impulses. They have kept their sense of peoplehood and tribalism. At times they take them seriously, and at other times they neglect them. But all in all, there is a recognition that, as Father John Courtney Murray has said, religious pluralism is the human condition. It is written into the script of history. Nowhere has it been so manifest or taken so seriously as in the United States, the pioneer and the parable for the modern world in that respect.

II. Experimentalism

While pluralism in religion has been at the heart of the tradition, experimentalism or the experimental spirit has been what has made it interesting. If less obvious, it is no less important. I consider it the basic element in the American experience of spirituality. When we use the word experiment, we refer to the fact that in religion, as in so many other respects, Americans are always ready with "Plan B." But "Plan B" is not argued on purely pragmatic grounds; it is seen to derive out of a consistent set of principles. There is always room for testing, for trying again, for changing.[4]

Are not all nations religiously experimental? Some of them may be turning toward this temper. Change is the law of life, and people can be dragged into it almost anywhere. But that change is usually slow and subtle, and yielded to grudgingly. It is important to look at characteristic ways of regarding religion elsewhere and in the past. In primitive religion the task was to adhere to the cosmos and the universe of meanings that were already given. The witch doctor, the shaman, and the priest all existed to monitor the ceremonies and ritual acts that grew out of a myth that explained the world. There was no thought of change, only of conformity. While biblical messianism should have meant change in the European world, that world which provided American ancestry, the establishment of Christianity in the fourth century and the forcing of Judaism into the ghetto (while Islam was kept at bay geographically), led people again to see religion as fixed, never to be tampered with. The European tradition of sociology of religion, because it converged, with Émile Durkheim, on "the elementary forms of religious life" or because it drew on Europe's traditionalist religious construct, tended to regard religion only as an apprehension of a given world.

Even Alexis de Tocqueville, that sophisticated observer of Amer-

---

[4] For an elaboration of experimentalism, see "Experiment in Environment," my paper in *The Journal of Religion*, July 1976. That article, several of whose highlights are condensed here, accents foreigners' perceptions of the American experimental sense.

ican variety and change, brought such assumptions with him. He believed that in the moral and religious world "everything is classified, systematized, foreseen and decided beforehand"; it was only in the political world that "everything is agitated, disrupted, and uncertain." Religion evoked "a passive though a voluntary obedience," while it was politics that inspired "an independence scornful of experience, and jealous of all authority." He did not believe that in the religious world things could be "agitated, disrupted, and uncertain . . . malleable, capable of being shaped and combined at will."[5]

Yet the American religious tradition *was* malleable. Change may be disguised under what sociologist J. Milton Yinger called "symbols of nonchange." "Changes are . . . obscured by the continuity of symbols."[6] That means that American religionists characteristically have had to refer to a script, to a code or canon. They have had to reassure themselves that their changes were in line with a past that had come to them by revelation. But in the context of that revelation were endless possibilities for adaptation and innovation. They might even despise the term "innovation"—as New Englanders in colonial times most certainly did. Then they innovated.

Jacques Maritain saw a carryover of experimentalism in all of American life. Americans embodied Hegel's "infinite elasticity" of the spirit, resilience and versatility. "At the origin of this *fluidity* there is the activity of the mind at work in the people. in the humble ways of daily life."

Americans seem to be in their own land as pilgrims, prodded by a dream. They are always on the move—available for new tasks, prepared for the possible loss of what they have. They are not settled, installed. . . . In this sense of becoming and impermanence one may discern a feeling of evangelical origin which has been projected into temporal activity.[7]

While in its Protestant versions experimentalism took on an optimistic and progressivist cast, the Catholics who came here, even if

5 Alexis de Toqueville, *Democracy in America* (New York: Vintage, 1954), Vol. I, 45f.

6 J. Milton Yinger, *Sociology Looks at Religion* (New York: Macmillan, 1963), pp. 70f.

7 Jacques Maritain, *Reflections on America* (New York: Scribners, 1958), pp. 37, 95f.

they still carried along some sense of fate and fixity, also were observed to be experimenters. George Santayana wrote that Catholicism "is ancient, metaphysical, poetic, elaborate, aescetic, autocratic, and intolerant. . . . Everything in American life is at the antipodes to such a system. Yet the American Catholic is entirely at peace. His tone is everything, even in religion, is cheerfully American."[8] Eric von Kuehnelt-Leddihn, the conservative Catholic, in 1950 was again and again "cheered by the American [Catholic] readiness and freshness in tackling organizational problems; the old pioneering spirit is far from dead."[9]

The word "experiment" courses through American religious history, from John Clarke's colonial support of its "lively experiment" in religious freedom, to Thomas Jefferson's "fair experiment" of separating religious and civil spheres, to Philip Schaff's observation that "voluntaryism" was the great "experiment" in church history, to Hilaire Belloc's concern lest Americans devise a kind of civil religion which would be its "experiment" with a new religion.[10] Jews saw America as their Zion; so did blacks.

Those experiments could not have gone on had not Americans come to regard their environment itself as being somehow revelatory and redemptive. The sense that God was working new things here, that, as Reverend John Robinson said in 1620, "the Lord hath more truth and light yet to break forth out of his holy Word," was possible because they took security from knowing that there *was* a Word. American experimentalism has not been mere pragmatism. In a snide passage the maverick European Marxist Ernst Bloch has written that "to understand Marxist practice and propaganda as well, we must hold fast to the view that something is true not because it is useful, but always because, insofar as, and to the degree that something is true, it is useful." He contrasted that to American bourgeois pragmatism, "which holds that the truth value of any

---

[8] George Santayana, *Character and Opinion in the United States* (Garden City, N.Y., 1956), p. 29.

[9] Quoted by Daniel Herr and Joel Wells, *Through Other Eyes* (Westminster, Md.: Newman, 1965), p. 204.

[10] See Sidney E. Mead, *The Lively Experiment* (New York: Harper and Row, 1963), pp. 25f., 59; Philip Schaff, *America: A Sketch of Its Political, Social, and Religious Character* (Cambridge, Mass.: Harvard, 1961), p. 213; for Hilaire Belloc, see Dan Herr and Joel Wells, *op. cit.*, pp. 97f.

knowledge is to be measured by its success—which brings profit and common utility—and that any truth apart from this bourgeois type oriented to profitability is impossible and senseless. This may be true in a country where everybody is a salesman, a seller of himself, but surely *this* kind of 'theory-practice' is useless for us."[11] There may be elements of such styles of bourgeois pragmatism in American religion, but over-all it must be said that every evidence shows that the people felt free to experiment because they felt that they were operating on the basis of a truth that would become utile because it was true. It was located in God's holy Word and in a benign environment.

Over against "Plan A" and against fate or fixity, Americans posed "Plan B," freedom, fluidity—experiment. Our history has been marked by positive and negative experiments, by innovations and revisions and reversals—all of them perceived by us to be in a continuity, making up a tradition. Our basic experience has been our own revolution in religion—the lively and fair experiment of religious freedom, the separation of Church and State, and "voluntaryism." Most of our subsequent experiments have been corollaries of the basic move and shift. Alexis de Tocqueville pondered it thus:

Two things are astonishing about America, the great changeableness of most human behavior and the singular fixity of certain principles. . . . Men living in democratic societies . . . are forever varying, altering, and restoring secondary matters, but they are very careful not to touch fundamentals. They love change, but they dread revolutions.[12]

Here Tocqueville was either blighted by his European concept of fixity or he did not notice that in religion America had had its revolution, or felt that it had. It had devised a new fundamental element on the basis of which a wide range of experiments was possible.

To some, this experimental attitude is deadening to the spirit. T. S. Eliot saw it as a disease, a passion:

> *The endless cycle of idea and action,*
> *Endless invention, endless experiment,*

11 Ernest Bloch, *On Karl Marx* (New York: Herder & Herder, 1971), p. 131.
12 *Oeuvres completes*, ed. by J. P. Mayer, Vol. I (2), pp. 262, 254, quoted in *New York Review of Books* (XXIIII, No. 1, Feb. 5, 1976), p. 6.

Brings knowledge of motion, but not of stillness;
Knowledge of speech, but not of silence;
Knowledge of words, and ignorance of the Word.[13]

Yet Americans believed that they were not ignoring the Word in their alterations. On its basis they came to convert the Indians—and then they removed or killed them, finding scriptural justification for the move. They both supported and abolished slavery in part on grounds of "the Word." They came to establish monolithic and monopolistic theocracies and developed diverse and pluralistic democracies in religion. They brought along with them and adapted and transformed all the faiths known to Europe, and some from Africa and Asia, but felt free to invent an astonishing new range of sects and cults. The Protestants developed ideology for empire and then yielded it to pluralist impulses. The courts argued that they themselves should be "wholesomely neutral" and then, after saying that our civil institutions presuppose a Supreme Being, limited the attention to that Being in public schools and allowed for conscientious objection as being sacred even if there is no reference to that Being in the mind of the objector. The Americans invented the denominational system and the voluntary pattern, lacking precedent for both. They changed their polities on the basis of both practical necessity and ecumenical encounter, and then went on to explain how the changed version was what God had had in mind all along. Fortunately for all of them in all these moves, their scriptures were sufficiently deep, obscure, and manifold to permit many interpretations and impulses!

III. SCRIPTURALISM

This whole discussion of experimentalism so far relied on a sense that American religious life was somehow pre-scripted. It was from a holy Word that God's further truth and light was to break. Jerald C. Brauer linked "a constant free experimentation and search for a fuller manifestation of God's truth and will" with "a sustained effort

[13] Chorus from *The Rock,* cited as epigraph by Daniel Bell in *The Cultural Contradictions of Capitalism* (New York: Basic, 1976), p. vii.

to avoid going beyond the truth and light already known in the Bible and codified in certain basic beliefs and confessions."[14] Such resort to the scripted and the codified went far beyond Protestantism.

It has often been pointed out that even in the radically non-Christian counterculture of the 1960's, young Americans who wanted to leave the Bible far behind were also scriptural people. The Hare Krishna youth hawk their scriptures in airports, and elaborate them endlessly. Sun Myung Moon's followers have their scriptures, just as do the Americans who have their versions of Maoism, with their thoughts of the party chairman. People who live in communes read the *Whole Earth Catalog* not as literary critics read a text, nor as aesthetes do for enjoyment, but as a kind of canon. So to move beyond the Bible does *not* mean to move beyond a scripture.

Scripturalism did first come to America, however, on biblical terms. Despite all the subsequent changes in our national life, nothing has displaced the Hebrew Scriptures and the New Testament from their positions of privilege. The antecedency helps; the people who give names to a culture hold power for an indefinite period. Americans may be increasingly biblically illiterate, but biblical lore is so bonded to their heritage that whenever they become thoughtful, whenever they reach deeply into their political lore (as with Abraham Lincoln) or into their literature (as with Nathaniel Hawthorne, or Herman Melville, or even William Faulkner), they are going to come across biblical nuances and promises.

The elites among the colonists were very explicit in stating that their lives were lived out as a new reading of the plot of books of Exodus and Exile. Christian though they were, they did not use the New Testament to set up their theocracies or their Bible commonwealths (as William Penn called his), because the New Testament's sense of an imminent end of the world limited its usefulness as code or canon for laws in the earthly city. For that reason, Jews have seldom had basic difficulty with the American legal or literary traditions. While America may be a *communitas communitatum,* a community whose subcommunities may disagree on the choice of scriptures or the content of the agreed-upon scriptures, the *communitas* itself has been marked by the scriptural and even biblical sense.

14 Jerald C. Brauer, *Protestantism in America* (Philadelphia: Westminster, 1965), p. 7.

From the scripturalism have come many *creencias* of American life. Among them are the notions that this is a nation "under God"; that this nation has been pushed into history, and is being pulled from the future, by the biblical God or by a Supreme or Kind Providence, or whatever; that America has a mission, a destiny. Dangerous ideas of chosenness those may all be, but they also endow the people with a sense of worth and value. America is "genetically programmed" to take the Bible relatively seriously. But even though biblical meanings are thinned out, attenuated, progressively forgotten, or transformed beyond recognizability, the scriptural sense is likely to live on. There is no mythical past, no given cosmology that gives life to the people. In the midst of pluralism, arguments and representations have to be made on the basis of texts that are endowed with sacred or normative status in the many subcultures.

IV. ENLIGHTENMENT

The Bible did not hold a unique position at the time of the birth of the nation, that moment from which so much later American life derives. For it happens that in the quarter-century surrounding the birth of the nation a new set of ideas had come to prominence. We refer to them as an "American Enlightenment." Europe, of course, had an Enlightenment at the same time, a more extensive, consistent, full-blown event. But the European Enlightenment ordinarily worked *against* religious claims and opposed the standard religious tradition. In America the Enlightenment was absorbed into the religious claims and either supported or had to coexist with the religion of the churches and subgroups.

In 1749 Benjamin Franklin, despairing of the churches' ability to get themselves together enough to give basis to the nation or to provide it with morals and virtue, spoke of "the necessity of a *Publick Religion*."[15] That public religion was grounded not simply in the Scriptures—though Franklin, Washington, Jefferson, and their kith and kind showed respect for them apart from their supernaturalism. Now religion was also to be grounded in social process, in a reason

[15] Donald H. Meyer, *The Democratic Enlightenment* (New York: G. P. Putnam's, 1976), pp. 3, 79.

and nature that were both accessible to all people of thought and good will or good intentions. Here was a modified Deism, a post-Christian style of religious philosophy. While it was soon countered by Protestant revivalists and Catholic or Jewish immigrants and fled from by secular folk who did not want to be identified with the excesses of the French Revolution, the Enlightenment did leave its stamp on American institutions. Taught as the truth about life by no known philosophy department in America, and seen as the creed in no church today, it still provided the basis for the nearest thing there is to a national creed—the Declaration of Independence—and was an element in the forming of the constitutional, legal, political, and educational systems in America. It provided the public with just enough hint of ideology to make it possible for them to adhere both to their particular faiths and the general ethos or code.

Earlier visitors were and modern commentators still are puzzled at American toleration, the ability of this people to combine almost fanatic faith in the creeds or ways propounded by separate groups with the relaxed faith in the ways of Enlightenment toleration, and public or generalized religion. Gustave de Beaumont, Tocqueville's traveling companion, admitted that he was puzzled:

As a matter of fact, nothing is commoner in the United States than this indifference toward the nature of religions, which doesn't however eliminate the religious fervour of each for the cult he has chosen. Actually, this extreme tolerance on the one hand towards religions in general—on the other this considerable zeal of each individual for his own religion, is a phenomenon I can't yet explain to myself. I would gladly know how a lively and sincere faith can get on with such a perfect toleration; how one can have equal respect for religions whose dogmas differ.[16]

Beaumont thought that was possible because of the superficiality of Americans' faiths, because they were broad but not deep. He was not wholly wrong. But he also overlooked the range of ways in which thoughtful and scholarly people have been able to combine their separate scriptures with Enlightenment universalism—or to see that

[16] Quoted in George Wilson Pierson, *Tocqueville in America* (Garden City, N.Y.: Doubleday, 1959), p. 70.

the Enlightenment itself was not universal, but was sometimes its own sect!

That Enlightenment ethos, whose detail never had much following, but whose outline remains strong in our institutions, is therefore seen in America to be a religious positive, even though in Europe it was regarded negatively, as a displacement of historic faith. In America the two kinds of faith are seen not as contradictory (which they sometimes are), but as complementary, overlapping, mutually supportive, and—in the minds of the most reflective—both grounded in a still deeper order of Being that may always elude mortals who in their finitude cannot reach its extent or depth. But from Fundamentalism to Unitarianism, in highly varied ways, Americans celebrate and live out many of the intentions of Enlightened religion.

V. VOLUNTARYISM

Were one able to separate the historical forms that the term "evangelical" connotes in America from its theological content, the word would be useful for describing an important element in the stamping of American religion. However, because evangelism refers to the Gospel of Jesus Christ, it would be inappropriate for application to Judaism and other non-Christian faiths in America. And though Roman Catholicism is devoted to that Gospel, Catholics would find the word too colored by Protestant history. Even within Protestantism the seizure and preemption of the term "evangelical" by a single sect renders it at least momentarily suspect even as a formal category.

For that reason I have chosen to characterize the American style of experience and affiliation as "voluntaryism." Note the "y." It is not *voluntarism*—"one or other theory or doctrine which regards will as the fundamental principle or dominant factor in the individual or in the universe" (*Oxford English Dictionary*). Voluntaryism, instead, is "the principle or tenet that the Church and educational institutions should be supported by voluntary contributions instead of by the State; any system which rests upon voluntary action or principles." The accent is on volunteering, not on the will. And while the dictionary definition accents the fiscal and legal implications, voluntaryism in America carries with it a heavy burden of assumptions about the personal agent and his religious experience along with reference to the character of the associations that are formed by the experiencers.

Included in the concept of voluntaryism is a competitive spirit. Daniel J. Boorstin has shown how encompassing such a spirit is, for it also includes Judaism, which has seen itself as being in no way missionary or evangelistic, nor given to advertising. Yet what Boorstin calls "Instrumentalism" has taken over. "Even Judaism—or at least its reformed branch—has become pretty well assimilated to this instrumental emphasis. One Jewish congregation has for the motto of its Sunday School, 'Sinai never does anything halfway.' "[17] When the revivalist calls the potential convert out of the world, he is not really asking the evangelized one to turn his back on it. He is offering a ticket to the "OK world," and is participating in a cultural initiation rite wherever evangelism has been pervasive.

The voluntary style is not necessary where there is no pluralism. There all citizens would be, virtually by the fact of birth, members of the single church. It is not plausible where there is no experimentalism, for it represents the opposite of the sense of fixity and fate that has characterized so much of what was called primitive and what was ancestral and is even now European religion. It draws on scripturalism, but scriptures are commended more "for the services they perform than for the truths they affirm," to use Boorstin's summary of the theme. (That is not to say the truths are not affirmed; they simply are not pushed forward as the main advantage for followers of a code or an invitation.) And voluntaryism draws heavily on the Enlightenment gift of toleration, for it assumes that, religiously, "any number can play," and that support for such playing exists in our law and ethos. Further, voluntaryists tend to rely on a second American Enlightened presupposition: that the separate churches can go about their business without disrupting the commonweal, that the various groups share enough ideas or beliefs to make possible a society, and not a jungle.

The Great Awakening of the eighteenth century may best be seen as the moment when the revolution toward voluntaryism occurred. From then until now the religion of experience has been

17 Daniel J. Boorstin, *The Genius of American Politics.* (Chicago: University of Chicago Press, 1953), p. 141.

somehow seen as more religious than is the religion of interpretation or action. Someone is *really* religious if he or she can cite and discourse upon a profound conversion experience, can engage in intense meditation or prayer, is especially devotional and attuned to the transcendent. Those features may not all be admired in the culture, but critics as well as apologists use them as marks for measuring and designating the truly religious. The Awakeners of the 1730's and 1740's and their successors ever since—including those in Catholicism—have stressed experiential religion. Some even called this experimental religion. They stressed the location of religion in the passions and the affections, the will and the emotions. Here was religion of heart and not just of mind and hand. Yet most previous religion was somehow heart religion. One could there and then go deeper in one's apprehension of an existing faith. But in America one first went deep in the art of choosing a faith. "Are you born again?"

While a communal context for experiential decision has always been applied, there is also something personal and even isolating about the voluntaryist appeal. "Do you accept Jesus Christ as your personal savior?" is a question somewhat different from the biblical ones, in which a person is saved with a people. But in America the covenantal community was always in the process of eroding, evaporating, being blurred, being reshaped. The evangelizer who called for voluntary decision called for a personal appropriation.

Voluntaryism's communal concept is also not so much a "given," as an *a priori,* a part of fate and fixity, a church that exists in the mind of God and the plan of the universe. No matter what the theology of the church may be, in America, where as H. L. Mencken observed, one "gets religion" and is enjoined to "go to the church of your choice," the religious organization is seen as in part a product of the sum total of conversions and choices. Theological exceptions abound, but the psychology and sociology of American religion strongly reinforce the voluntaryistic outlook.

THE AMERICAN TOMORROW

It remains to revisit the five themes and look briefly at their prospects. The American resolution as I have described its tradition is fragile, delicate, veneer-thin, gossamer, and possibly ephemeral. Experiments in social forms tend to have those characteristics. Two main choices lie ahead. On the one hand, our citizens may continue to pursue loneliness and drift from vestigial senses of community into religious isolation. Religion becomes only what one does with his solitariness. It is "doing one's own thing," "doing it my way," inventing "do-it-yourself" syntheses. Thomas Luckmann, in *The Invisible Religion*, has depicted such a tendency as normative in industrialized societies, where mobility and media prevent people from finding support for their belief and behavior in their primary and secondary associations. That invisible religion is the religion of the high-rise apartment, the faith of the television dial-twister who selects the evangelist of his choice, subscribes to a mail-order faith, visits the friendly neighborhood astrologer, and the like.

The other extreme, which strikes me as a kind of mild Maoism in religion, would rise out of despair over the alienation and anomie engendered by religious individualism. It would come as an ideology that would explain and reinforce post-republican and post-capitalist turns in the larger society. Robert Heilbroner typically foresees such a religion being generated as the business civilization drifts toward the planned economy.

I suspect that a major force for the transformation of business civilization will be a new religious orientation, directed against the canons and precepts of our time, and oriented toward a wholly different conception of the meaning of life and a mode of social organization congenial to the encouragement of that life.

. . . A high degree of political authority will be inescapable in the period of extreme exigency we can expect a hundred years hence. This augurs for the cultivation of nationalist, authoritarian attitudes, perhaps today foreshadowed by the kind of religious politicism we find in China. The deification of the state, whatever we may think of it from the standpoint of our still-cherished individualist philosophies, seems therefore the most likely replacement for the deification of materialism that is the unacknowledged religion of our business culture.[18]

18 For these two choices see Thomas Luckmann, *The Invisible Religion* (New York: Macmillan, 1967); and Robert L. Heilbroner, *Business Civilization in Decline* (New York: W. W. Norton, 1976), pp. 119f.

That religion of the state would be an extension of Franklin's "*Publick Religion*" or Bellah's "civil religion" at the expense of the separate faiths. The "invisible" choice would issue in an almost desperate experimentalism (for which the 1970's give considerable precedent), an atomization of pluralism, a continuing accent on scripturalism, an exploitation of Enlightenment presuppositions, and fulfilled voluntaryism. The collectivist alternative would mean the move toward a final experiment, the end of effective pluralism, the development of a new scripture or selection of a single old one, a despair of Enlightenment toleration, and the closing off of voluntaryist styles. I am not predicting that either will prevail. In the short term, the individualizing types are stronger, while it is in the longer range that many foresee the collectivizing system becoming attractive to greater numbers of leaders and people.

Experimentalism. For the moment, Americans remain poised between the two resolutions of their two centuries (and more) old approach to religion. As Dwight Eisenhower might have put it, "Things are more like they are now than they ever were before." The people are free to set up shop and hang out a shingle for any religion, faith, superstition, or magical system ever known to man—or to try to cancel out them all. They are able to do that because of the security they continue to draw from their environment, which, even in our secular era, is still perceived as having at least vestiges of promise, possibilities of revelatory power. Trying and testing go on.

Adaptation is as strong among the new groups as it is among the old. Hare Krishna proponents wear wigs in airports in order to accommodate themselves to prospects who might be put off by too much exoticism. The Black Muslims, only months after their founder's death, invited the white Beautiful People to their parties, even though to them whites had represented the devil a year earlier. Transcendental Meditation turns commercial and secular, leaving behind its Hindu roots but still offering quasi-religious benefits. The Jesus freaks turn straight and square. Pentecostalists and charismatics call for spontaneity and then write guide books for precision at prayer meetings and try to install authoritarian disciplinary systems. So the environment works its magnetic and erosive effects at once, while new groups and new emphases constantly keep appearing to offer still different ways for American spirituality. That experimentalism, however, verges on the atomism of "invisible religion" and has diminish-ing social effect. It would hardly be useful to the magistrates who might seek a religion for cementing new social bonds. So its future is not wholly assured.

Pluralism. In the immediate American tomorrow there seems to be no threat of a diminution of pluralism. *Ex uno plures* has been the religious model of recent years, as a new denominationalism and a new ethnicism in religion have inspired tribal thoughts and practices. The calls for a civil religion or a resuscitated "religion of the repub-lic" represented attempts to bring some order to the chaos in the early 1960's, but they were followed by new chaos and effervescence later in the decade. What seems necessary is the development of pub-licly accessible theories and theologies by which pluralists can ground their particular faiths in some sort of universal, ways by which they can relate their peculiarities to something general. Otherwise there will be only tribal soliloquies and solipsism and the death of the *com-munitas communitatum.*

Scripturalism. The standard question that ensues when biblical back-grounds to American culture are discussed is this: what will happen to the substance of the vision as the years pass? The schools are in-creasingly secularized, the Sunday schools fail in promulgating bibli-cal traditions, the home has broken down as a teaching agency. How will a new generation be shaped around even the mere reminiscences of biblical patterns and thoughts? Will not America seek a "new myth," a new set of symbols? Why has not the boom in Bible transla-tions and sales resulted in an increase of either biblical literacy or the restoration of biblical impulses in the public sectors of life?

If the Bible becomes ever more a sediment and a residue in American ideologies, it remains to be stirred up and activated. But though the biblical impetus has been diminishing, scripturalism seems to have a future, and would be assured whether America took a turn toward more individualism or more collectivism, toward more pluralism or more homogeneity. There seems to have to be a textual reference point for believers in the midst of the storms of modernity.

Enlightenment. As a formal philosophy, Enlightenment is in diffi-culty. The professional philosophers tend to disdain it: its language does not "check out." Many theological revivals among biblical faiths since mid-century have called its naturalism into question. The irrationalisms of an existentialist age counter its reasonableness. Lacking fresh articulation, it survives chiefly because of the way it made public institutions legitimate. As Sidney E. Mead once remarked, in an indelicate but apt phrase, Americans, especially the evangelicals, have had to swallow the Enlightenment's ideas in order to buy into its system, but they have been able neither to digest nor to regurgitate them.

But if the substantive philosophy of the Enlightenment is eclipsed, the formal cast remains as a set of intentions voiced in Walter Lippmann's "public philosophy," Father John Courtney Murray's attempt to transcend mere pluralism, Reinhold Niebuhr's ironic vision of American history, and the like. That public philosophy lacks widely recognized proponents today, and its liberal version is hardly visible. A moderately conservative call for tradition and continuity recalling some of its principles is present in the writings of Daniel Bell, Robert Nisbet, and others who are concerned about the loss of intention and authority in culture.

If the public philosophy is not regularly voiced with clarity and power in public, it is in even worse shape in the religious organizations. There the experiential prevails, and little premium has been placed on reason. Many an apocalyptic pitch in popular religion is a thinly disguised call for a new Dark Age.

Voluntaryism. In the short range, it is hard to see a disappearance of the experiential note that is basic to voluntaryism. There are signs that the frantic and even faddish lust for experience is diminishing. But if people wish to be religious tomorrow, it is likely that they will use their religion as a sphere in which they can have experiences that metropolitan and technological life ordinarily deny them. There is a new personalism and intimacy in the therapies and "small group movements" that have characterized religion for some years. And voluntary associational instincts are likely to remain strong. But those trends are qualified both by the attractions of the "pursuit of loneliness" and the "invisible religion" on one hand and the homogenizing corporate style of civil religions on the other.

The script for the future, then, breathes very much the sense of what I have here characterized as the American tradition. It is seen as a process and not a product, a stewardship based not on a belief in progress, but on a recognition that the alternatives are less promising. "The authority of the eternal yesterday," as Max Weber called it, has never been consuming in America. But after two hundred years it is being heard among other authorities. Not all who invoke it do so in order to settle argument, to lay upon society the dead hand of the past. Many see in it the basis for better disagreements than those we have known, livelier debates, and some measure, at least, of freedom.

VII

NEWTON N.
MINOW [1]

ELECTRONICS

AND

Your morning news appears on a wall-size screen attached to your home communicenter. A video printout of the day's schedule of movies, sports, and lessons appears, subject to your choice, and you adjust the programming to meet your interests and time preferences. You set a timer to record programs or lessons you desire to keep on hand; in the meantime microfilm you ordered from a foreign data bank arrives. When it is time for your prearranged date with your Australian chess opponent, his moves appear on your screen just as yours appear on his.

You shop for clothes and food by viewing the merchandise on your communicenter, ordering them with your computercard, which

[1] Credit is gratefully acknowledged by Newton N. Minow to his daughter Martha Minow, a student at Yale Law School, for her research and valued assistance in preparing this lecture.

THE

FUTURE

automatically records the transactions with your bank. You participate in a town meeting through the two-way video of your communicenter, expressing your opinion and votes on the current proposals.
Your doctor scans your vital functions via electronic attachments to
your communicenter, and then connects you with a specialist at the
Mayo Clinic who explains a new treatment to you.

By dialing central data banks, you obtain printouts and video
cassette programs on recent scientific experiments, theological papers,
legal cases—anything you would like to study. You dictate a letter to
be sent anywhere, or talk with anyone on your videoscreen. Pictorial,
graphic, sound, and print media become one whole center, opening
up all sources of knowledge to you as well as serving as vehicles for
your own personal communication.

Far out speculations on the distant future? No indeed; those
were speculations twenty years ago. Now they are technological re-

ality. Videophones, microfilm, videotape, wall-size screens, dial information banks—they all exist and are gaining in usage. The problems which remain are those of economics, costs, and marketing. When they are solved, the new world of electronic communications will further dominate our lives. The technology is already here.

But let us pause to heed James Thurber's warning about the speed of changing technology: "Man is flying too fast for a world that is round. Soon he will catch up to himself in a great rear-end collision and many will never know that what hit him from behind was man."

Too often we allow changes to happen simply because they seem to be logical fulfillments of existing trends. At this national Bicentennial, and this institution's Centennial, we have good reason to pause, to reflect, to recognize the implications of change in technology and communications. For if we do not align change with what we value, we will simply value change.

"Electrons have no morals. They serve free men and dictators with equal fervor. Their use in transmitting human ideas depends on those who design the machines and control their use, and in the United States this ultimately will depend on the general public." So wrote Ben Bagdikian, scholar of the new information technology. How will the changing techniques of communication affect the ways in which we see ourselves and our world? Will they foster the freedom of expression crucial to the survival of a creative democracy? Or will they manipulate and restrict individual communication? Will the media bring information and culture down to the lowest common denominator? Will Orwell's dread prophecies for 1984, less than a decade away, come true? Or will new technology challenge and elevate human senses and sensibilities? Let us examine those questions in the hope that we will direct electronics rather than simply take electronic directions.

First we need some broad historical perspective. If we remember that "what is past is prologue," we will understand how previous changes in communications technology and information dissemination revolutionized society. When Marshall McLuhan said that "the medium is the massage" he gave us a valuable, if often misunderstood, insight: the way in which information is conveyed often touches and instructs us as much as the content of the message itself does. As we shall see, the message of technological change in communications has been increased knowledge and dispersed power, bringing an expansion in sophistication, education, and democracy. If we perceive the meaning and manner of previous transitions, we can identify those directions we value, make moral judgments, and choose wisely among new alternatives.

All of us know that new tools and materials significantly change the life-styles and concerns of a society. When ancient Egyptian rulers first started to write on papyrus rather than on clay tablets, messages suddenly became portable; a king's power could extend over a greater area. But that expanded authority had to be shared with the copyists and the papyrus-makers. Erik Barnouw, America's foremost historian of communications, has concluded that "All this meant a shift away from absolute monarchy, a dispersal of authority that is said to have penetrated deeply into Egyptian life. Papyrus begat bureaucracy."

Centuries later, paper was produced outside of the church monopoly of the Middle Ages, replacing parchment. New technological changes culminated with the invention of movable type. The introduction of movable type democratized learning, shared knowledge, expanded faith in the dignity and reason of the common man, and was an enormous force in the Renaissance and the Reformation. That change in technique allowed mass production to spread classical knowledge, and also supported the business and the vernacular of a new merchant class. The printing press spread the power of thought and creativity. Ideas took on new energy as they were sent more quickly and farther than they had ever traveled before.

With the expanded movement of information and ideas came social mobility and massive social changes. Custodians of tradition, of course, resisted those changes; in 1671, the Governor of Virginia expressed his thanks to God that the printing press, breeder of heresy and disobedience, had not yet arrived in his colony. But no longer could knowledge belong solely to the clergy or royalty; the technological change in communications had advanced social change toward democracy.

In the 1800's, technology in the form of the camera and the telegraph allowed even more dramatic sharing of experiences. New methods of communication transmitted ideas more vividly and more quickly than had ever been thought possible. Suddenly "news" really meant what was new and immediate. Suddenly people had knowledge in their hands of social changes across the globe. New information bolstered faith in their own power to overthrow tyranny and to launch mass politics. By the 1870's, the phonograph was bringing new entertainment inside homes, the telephone was introducing connections between homes, and more and more people were communicating with each other.

In 1901 the *New National Dictionary* defined the word "broadcast" as the "act or process of scattering seeds." A quarter of a century later, the *New Century Dictionary* defined it as "to scatter or desseminate, specifically, radio messages, speeches, etc." In the space of those two decades, the new seeds being scattered were the impulses of radio. But the change was much more profound than a mere change in dictionary definitions.

When radio broadcasting began in 1920 after decades of inventions and experiments, it created popular personalities, brought the voice of the President into every household, and in a little more than a decade was communicating the personality as well as the policies of Franklin Delano Roosevelt. Radio developed new trends in music. It made possible instantaneous transmission of breaking news stories. In 1925, an American and an Englishman, independently, were experimenting with combining radio techniques with new discoveries in photography and optics, using a scanning disc, vacuum tubes, and photoelectric cells. Refinements in technology proceeded rapidly, and experimental television stations were operating by 1930. Broadcasting development was delayed during World War II, but television reappeared in 1946 and it instantly captured the public's imagination.

By 1947, some 14,000 homes had television sets, and Americans were watching regular shows such as "Meet the Press," "Kukla, Fran and Ollie," and "Howdy Doody." Five million American families were tuning in their sets in 1950. By 1960, the number had soared to 45 million. Today more families have television sets than bathtubs. More than half the homes in America have color television. In 1976 the New York State Assembly voted that a family's television set was such a basic necessity that it could not be taken by creditors when possessions were seized to satisfy debts. People spent more time watching the tube than they did attending church, school, concerts—more time than in any single activity other than sleeping. Sixty per cent of American families changed their sleeping patterns because of television schedules. Fifty-five per cent changed their mealtimes, and 78 per cent use television as an electronic babysitter. In large cities, plumbing systems had to be redesigned to accommodate heavy use of water during prime time commercials. But besides changing the habits of viewers, television modified the nature of entertainment and information transmission. Knowledge and experiences previously restricted to the few are now available to everyone.

Television is our national mass medium. Its power is too comprehensive to be measured. Capable of familiarizing any viewer with the mannerisms of a presidential candidate, the trivia of a game show, the excitement of a superbowl, the expressions of Groucho Marx, television has been accused of everything. Some believe that it creates unrest by showing prosperity to the poor. Others believe that it ended a war by bringing it into everyone's living room. Televising the McCarthy hearings, the Kennedy-Nixon debates, the Watergate hearings, and the political conventions brought government and politics to the entire nation, creating a shared experience. In fact, television has given us new powers of mobilizing public opinion. The development of the mass media correlates almost exactly with the growth of an industrial society, a society increasingly urban and then suburban, undergoing changes more rapidly than any previous time in history. Television offers outlets for joy and grief, an antidote to loneliness, a companion in an era when old rituals have lost their meanings.

We all identify President Kennedy's assassination and funeral with television. The launching of a space mission, a walk on the moon, a committee vote on impeachment—we were there, through television. Elderly and handicapped people keep in touch with current events and trends through television in a society which otherwise ends to ignore them. The mass nature of the media creates instant national heroes, national failures, memories, and rituals, weaving new webs of social cohesion.

Television, in the opinion of thoughtful social scientists, also alters the viewers' perception of events. Every microphone and camera becomes linked to the nervous system of the observer, extending the areas of exploration behind the scenes, beyond the moon. Television blurs distinctions between what is formal and informal, news and entertainment, foreign and familiar. Sitting in the same chair, dressed in the same attire, the viewer can see a religious service, a soap opera, a gangster chase scene, a situation comedy, a newscast, and a wrestling match. Reducing the special quality of certain events but increasing the importance of others, the television camera democratizes experiences as it carries them to our homes.

Where printed or written languages imposed a linear one-step-at-a-time transmission of ideas, television—along with film—carries complexity and simultaneity once possible only in face-to-face communication. Social scientists say that the visual media reaches a different hemisphere of the brain than the one used in written communication. Lloyd Morrisett of the Markle Foundation noted:

> *Words can transmit knowledge about values, attitudes and sensibilities but the values, attitudes or sensibilities themselves are something apart from and different from knowledge about them. . . . Choosing a verbal model for the transmission of knowledge has meant some inherent loss in the capacity to transmit other qualities. . . . [W]here words alone convey only poorly the excitement, fear and sudden rush of the stomach onto the throat from a ride on a roller coaster, a superwide screen and associated sound effects can do it very well.*

The same holds for the drama of a presidential resignation speech, an Olympics competition, a fire, a vote of the House Judiciary Committee.

A friend, visiting Los Angeles from West Germany, drove along the freeways. He noticed that every home, whether an apartment building or a house, a mansion or a tenement, had a television antenna poking up from its rooftop. He told me that the television antennas were like periscopes, enabling the people inside to see and hear what was going on outside. The metaphor is not only vivid, but also precise; television has become the sensory equipment of our era, involving perception powers; it allows us to peer where we have not been before, enabling all of us inside to see what is going on outside.

Yet if television enables all of us inside to see what is happening outside, does it also enable us to *understand* what is going on outside? Have we learned how to use and to harness this miraculous medium in a free and open society? Have we learned to use it to advance the democratic process, the cause of justice, the causes of social and moral development; the enlightenment of the mind and the heart?

As of 1976, we have not found the answers to these questions. The task for the remaining years in this century is to deepen the search for the answers, and to get more people involved in the search. I plead especially that our religious and academic leaders participate to a far greater degree than they have in the past. And I pose to you, briefly, two particular questions which need answers based on ethical and moral values. Those questions deal with the role of television in politics, and the role of television in changing our constitutional system.

In this election year, candidates for the presidency of the United States travel around the country, speaking to small groups of people, quickly and in slogans. They are barely perceived by the electorate. In this two hundredth year of our adventure and experiment with self-government, we have a powerful medium which can bring the candidates and the issues into every home. Yet it is not being used to enlighten and inform. Instead, we have sixty-second, thirty-second, and even ten-second commercials.

The United States Supreme Court, in the landmark decision of *Buckley v. Valeo,* had some important things to say about the First Amendment and politics in 1976. The Court said, "The First Amendment's protection against governmental abridgement of free expression cannot properly be made to depend on a person's financial ability to engage in public discussion." It also said that "The electorate's increasing dependence on television, radio, and other mass media for news and information has made these expensive modes of communication indispensable instruments of effective political speech."

What the Supreme Court said is well known to each of us. Most Americans now receive most of their news from television, and most form their political opinions and judgments because of what they see and hear on television and radio. Yet we have a system which too often bars access to the electorate except on terms of payment of vast sums of money. True, public funds are now available—but the disadvantages of the use of public funds under present arrangements in political campaigns offer major hazards to freedom.

Some years ago I was asked to chair a bipartisan commission, organized by the Twentieth Century Fund, to examine ways and means to use television more effectively in the process of choosing a President. Our commission, after a year's intensive study, unanimously recommended that the Congress of the United States change the rules. Legislation was introduced in the Congress, hearings were held—and nothing happened.

We said in our report, seven years before the Supreme Court's decision, that the electorate should have the opportunity to see and hear all significant candidates so that it could better judge their positions and personal qualities. We also said that such access of voters to a candidate should not depend exclusively on his ability to raise campaign funds. Therefore, we recommended that each significant presidential candidate and his running mate be given broadcast time simultaneously on all television and radio stations in the United States. The time would be called Voter's Time, and the programs would be designed to promote rational political discussion and involve live appearances by the candidates. We proposed that the federal government buy the time, at half price, from the broadcasters to reimburse their costs, and we found that six half-hours of radio and television time on every station in the country, in the six weeks before a Presidential election, would involve an expense of about $4 million every four years—or less than it would cost to mail a single post card to all voters.

Incumbents did not particularly like our idea, because it treats their opponents equally. Lethargy, inertia, and apathy were our foes. A few years went by, and then Watergate lighted the fires of reform. But that simple idea—the proposal that we link modern electronics to the political process—that simple, inexpensive idea, was not adopted.

My point is not that our proposal for Voter's Time is the panacea to solve America's problems for the last quarter of this century. My point is that religious and academic leaders of this nation were identified not with searches for solutions, but instead with the familiar forces of inertia, lethargy, and apathy, which are the most effective enemies of the democratic process. Adlai E. Stevenson, my old law partner, once said:

Participating in government in a democracy does not mean merely casting a ballot on election day. It means much more than that. It means an attitude, a moral view, and a willingness to assume a day-to-day responsibility. Too many say, "Politics is dirty"—and that is about their only protest about the quality of government—and far more use the word "politician" as a term of opprobrium, disrespect, and dishonor—and this in the land of Washington, Jefferson and Lincoln. . . .

I would remind you of an axiom of political science: People get the kind of government they deserve. Your public servants serve you right. Our American government may be defined, perhaps, as the government that really cares about the people. Just so, our government demands, it depends upon, the care and devotion of the people.

Today, the care and devotion of the people is directed at the television set in their home. Television, like their public servants, serves them right, and gives them the kind of politics on television which they deserve.

Let us turn now to another example of television's effect on our system, our governmental and constitutional system. Sometimes we amend our Constitution without knowing it. Constitutional Amendments are made imperceptibly, through technological change. For some years I have believed that, in the case of television, that has already happened, because we have altered the political boundaries of the country—its cities, boroughs, counties, and states.

Television signals spread out in circles, and each covers a circle whose run is about 60 to 75 miles from the transmitter. Cities and counties and states were marked by boundaries long before television existed, but today they bear little, if any, relationship to communications boundaries. If we were starting the United States of America in 1976 instead of 1776, we could all learn important lessons from the business community, which, when television arrived twenty-five years ago, redrew the boundaries of America with a television boundary line called a television market, or an "ADI"—an "area of dominant influence."

The advertising and marketing people, not a constitutional convention, divided the United States into 207 ADI's. Let us examine what this means in the case of New York, our most troubled large city.

Paul L. Klein, who is not a political scientist, but a New York City student of television, has observed that those who would solve New York City's problems ought not accept the city as Rand McNally defines it. Klein wrote:

The boundaries between boroughs, villages, towns, cities, counties, and states were first drawn when the Dutch were running things here. They were negotiated by people who owned the land. They were boundaries of convenience—often highly visible and unambiguous, like say, the Hudson River—and they made sense then. The same boundaries are useless today. Worse than useless. They obscure the nature of our problems, and they impede solutions by distracting us.

Thus, in the case of New York, if you measured by television signal boundaries, New York City would not be poor. Instead, it would encompass 18.2 million people, not 7.8 million, with an effective buying—and taxing—income of $94.4 billion, not $37.4 billion. The people who fled to the suburbs and outlying areas—who view the same television news program each evening as the people in the city and who comprise the same basic political community—would be a part of the solution instead of part of the problem.

Television signals know only electronic boundaries, not traditional geographic ones. The people within the circle of a television signal comprise a more sensible community of common interests than the archaic boundaries drawn before modern communications technology. Yet we persist in not adapting to technological change. Jefferson once wrote that while he did not favor frequent changes in laws and constitutions, we had to change as circumstances changed, for otherwise we would require a grown man to wear a coat which fit him when he was a young boy. Were Jefferson here today, and were he to examine television's effect on American life, would he want us to have ADI's instead of states?

These are the issues which should be under close scrutiny in 1976—the effect of television on politics and our constitutional system. These are issues which should have the guidance of our moral and ethical philosophers, our intellectual and religious leaders. Television is far too important to be left to the broadcasters themselves, to the FCC, to the politicians. Television today has redrawn the political landscape of the nation. Our institutions, our Congress, and our political parties have failed to reflect those alterations; they are still frozen in the structure of another era.

As an American Jew, deeply concerned about my country and my faith, I ask you to help find direction for electronics, rather than continue to take electronic direction. We need now to find new ways for our networks to link people's hearts together, rather than to divide them. I ask you, in this center of moral values, to address yourselves thoughtfully to these issues. The Jewish people, throughout history, have been known as the People of the Book. That is because only books were around when Judaism began. If Judaism were to begin today, in today's technology, we would be the people of television, radio, film—for Jews from Sarnoff and Goldwyn to Paley and Goldenson have been the exciting pioneers in all the new media of communication. But our rabbis and teachers still direct their concentration of Jewish moral and ethical values toward books—and the printed word.

During the Watergate crisis, America's attention, as was to be expected, was aimed at the television tube. Two members of the clergy were on television regularly—Rabbi Korff and Father McLaughlin, both defenders of President Nixon. The picture most Americans saw and heard in their homes was of church leaders on the wrong side of what was essentially a moral issue. Why? Where were the prophets in this era of electronics?

In today's world we must be more than the People of the Book. Martin Buber, whose passion for books was boundless, once wrote:

If I had been asked in my early youth whether I preferred to have dealings only with men or only with books, my answer would certainly have been in favour of books. In later years, this has become less and less the case. Not that I have had so much better experiences with men than with books; on the contrary, purely delightful books even now come my way more often than purely delightful men. But the many bad experiences with men have nourished the meadow of my life as the noblest book could not do, and the good experiences have made the earth into a garden for me. . . .

How I wish we could ask him about television! For television is a mixture of men and books, and its importance in our lives today and tomorrow is what nuclear fission is to conventional weapons. I believe that Buber would teach us to take television much more seriously in the next twenty-five years than we have in the past. And that we bring to television a sense of values and moral purpose.

Television is, after all, the most powerful means of communication in the history of the world. It will not diminish in its power. It will increase, and it is truly America's ADI—our areas of dominant influence. And it will not wait. For as Edward R. Murrow once said of television:

This instrument can teach, it can illuminate; yes it can even inspire. But it can do so only to the extent that humans are determined to use it to those ends. Otherwise, it is merely lights and wires in a box.

A week before he was assassinated, President Kennedy told one of his favorite stories, one which we should ponder at this Centennial and Bicentennial occasion. French Marshall Lyautey walked one morning through his garden with his gardner. He stopped at a certain point and asked his gardener to plant a tree there the next morning. The gardener said, "But the tree will not bloom for one hundred years." Marshall Lyautey looked at him and replied, "In that case, you had better plant it this afternoon."

VIII

JOHN B. OAKES

THE

RESPONSIBILITY

Above the entrance to the great building housing the National Archives of the United States is carved the inscription

WHAT IS PAST IS PROLOGUE

Embedded in that phrase is the key to any meaningful celebration this year of the two-hundredth anniversary of the setting of the corner-stone of American freedom, for it is out of the actions and aspirations of the past that man constructs his hopes and sets his goals for the future.

What is past is prologue; but though we are conditioned by the past, we cannot and must not be bound by it. The spirit of innovation and development within the continuum of history, intimately

OF THE PRESS

linked to the past but looking always toward the future, is the driving force of every human institution, without which it would atrophy and wither away.

It seems particularly fitting to me that the Hebrew Union College, which exemplifies so well the principle of progressive thought firmly based on the experience and philosophy of the ages, should be linking its own Centennial celebration with the nation's Bicentennial and, in doing so, examining some of the forces that have most deeply affected American life in the past two hundred years and are sure to continue to do so in the foreseeable future. One of those basic forces is the American press, whose origins and development are intimately intertwined with the history of our country from its very beginnings.

In the pre-Revolutionary period the press was already flourishing, and it had a major part to play in the formation of public opinion. The hyper-active American press helped shape the political evolution of the colonies toward independence, and, in the post-Revolutionary era in particular, it played an especially important role in the fierce struggle over adoption of the Constitution and in the Federalist–Anti-Federalist rivalry that followed. With the growth of political consciousness throughout this period went the intensification of political comment; and it was no accident that the long struggle for freedom that preceded and followed the Declaration of Independence was accompanied by a concurrent crescendo of efforts to establish a free—if not necessarily responsible—press.

In fact, by the time the first newspaper in all the Northwest Territories, the *Centinel,* was founded in this village of Cincinnati by a printer named William Maxwell—in a log cabin at the corner of Front and Sycamore Streets in the year 1793—the American press was probably the freest and certainly the most free-swinging in the world. It was sometimes corrupt, often courageous, frequently scurrilous, usually partisan, and always lively.

That was in striking contrast to the situation a century earlier, when America's first newspaper—the *Publick Occurrences* of Boston—was suppressed by the Governor after only one issue because, he said, its "sundry doubtful and uncertain reports" had been published "without the least Privity or Countenance of Authority." Its more cautious and longer-lived successor, the Boston *News-Letter,* carefully exhibited under its title the significant legend "Published by Authority"—which undoubtedly accounts for the fact that it, the first true American newspaper, lasted for nearly three-quarters of a century—until the Revolution ended both its authority and its existence.

Authority—that was the touchstone of the American press for its first hundred, colonial years; and it was to throw off the shackles of this authority that the editors of the pre-Revolutionary period increasingly devoted their attention, along with their parallel and closely related effort to achieve ever-increasing independence from the political authority of the British Crown.

Press freedom and political freedom went hand in hand; yet it is curious that neither the Declaration of Independence itself nor the Constitution of the United States, made any mention of that freedom of the press which had in fact contributed so heavily to the success of the Revolution and was so deeply imbedded in the libertarian philosophy of Jefferson and Madison. That deficiency was soon remedied by the First Amendment, but not before Hamilton had expressed in Federalist 84 these prescient words of caution, which, as we shall see, may have some application today:

What signifies a declaration that "the Liberty of the Press shall be inviolably preserved"? What is the Liberty of the Press? . . . Its security, whatever fine declaration may be inserted in any Constitution respecting it, must altogether depend on public opinion, and in the general spirit of the people *and the Government. (Emphasis added.)*

Even Hamilton could hardly have realized how deeply the press could come to be affected by "the general spirit of the people and the Government" and how, reciprocally, the people and the government could be affected in later generations, by a responsible, or an irresponsible, press.

It may help us to put the question in perspective if we remember that from the very earliest days of the Republic, the guarantee of freedom written into the Constitution with the First Amendment carried with it no guarantee, expressed or implied, of responsibility or restraint on the part of editors and publishers. That tradition of total freedom of expression was established with the very birth of the nation. No American in public life before or since suffered more from an unrestrained and intolerant press than Washington himself, though he firmly resolved, as he said, to pass over the calumnies against him in utter silence—and pass them over he did, at least in public. But it was not only personal abuse that Washington endured; it was also breaches—or alleged breaches—of security. It is instructive—in light of the contest between government and press today—to note that the very first President who was plagued by the leakage of secret information was not Gerald Ford or Lyndon Johnson, but George Washington. The problem of governmental secrecy versus press freedom in this democracy began at least as early as 1795, and it has not been resolved to this very day.

John Jay, Chief Justice of the United States, had signed his famous (or, if you were an Anti-Federalist in those days, infamous) Treaty with England, providing for final British evacuation of the Northwest Territories; but President Washington, knowing that the Treaty was sure to be bitterly opposed as too lenient by the francophile opposition, kept the terms of the Treaty temporarily secret, and the text of it locked up in his desk. However, in one of the more noted journalistic coups of the era, the Treaty was leaked to the virulently Anti-Federalist editor Benjamin Franklin Bache, who published its terms and text in what Washington must surely have considered an act of extreme political partisanship involving gross violation of the national security. Yet Bache continued to publish his Philadelphia *Aurora* as before, and continued to vilify Washington as before, in these words (among others):

If ever a nation was debauched by a man, the American nation has been debauched by Washington. . . . If ever a nation was deceived by a man, the American nation has been deceived by Washington. . . . Let his conduct . . . serve to be a warning that no man may be an idol.

Even the pamphleteer Tom Paine, Washington's former friend and admirer, was so outraged by the Jay Treaty that he too pushed his talent for scurrility to the outermost limits. This is part of his public letter to the long-suffering President:

And as to you, sir, treacherous in private friendship . . . and a hypocrite in public life, the world will be puzzled to decide, whether you are an apostate or an imposter, whether you have abandoned your principles; or whether you ever had any.

Yet, in the face of what must have seemed, at the very minimum, infringements of Executive privilege and of the bounds of propriety by such "infamous scribblers," as Washington privately called them, in what must have looked to the shaky, newborn government of the United States as total press irresponsibility and breaches of national security, the First Amendment stood firm. It was the basic principle of freedom of expression of speech and press, the bedrock on which American political democracy was built and rests today. The subsequent, if momentary, aberration of the Alien and Sedition Acts proved by their short life and the general revulsion against them (in which Washington joined) that such restrictions on freedom of speech and press were totally unacceptable to a free people. No one ever put it better than Thomas Jefferson, who himself suffered bitter attacks at the hands of the opposition press throughout his presidency: "Our liberty depends upon freedom of the press, and that cannot be limited without being lost."

In the nearly two hundred years since Jefferson wrote those words, the character and composition of the American press has undergone monumental changes. As its literary quality has declined, its newsgathering and news dissemination achievements have increased; if it has lost too much in individuality, it has gained too much in homogeneity. But with it all, it has remained free.

Today, as we enter our third century as a nation, we have come to a new time of testing. While the forms remain more or less the same, the relationship between citizen and government has changed; government at every level has inevitably become more remote from the individual citizen, and the individual citizen in turn has become more remote from government. Our country has been experiencing economic, political, social, and world convulsions whose effects are as yet only dimly understood; but one of those effects surely has been a new questioning of government and of government's ability to meet the needs and desires of the people within the essentially democratic framework.

We do not yet know what will be the ultimate result of the massive changes we have been witnessing in our domestic social and political structure in recent years: movement of the underclass out of America's rural areas into the slums of its cities; exodus of the middle class and the affluent to suburbia; disappearance of the family farm, and even to some degree of the family; increasingly strident demands of the dispossessed; exacerbation of tension between the races; destruction of the environment and misuse of those ultimate resources, the air, the water, and the land; unforeseen shortages in the supply of energy; startlingly new possibilities that there may be finite limits to economic growth.

In this short period of less than a quarter-century, our society has

been riven by a convulsion of mores on the part of a younger generation; our economy has plunged from affluence into severe unemployment, depression, and inflation; our position in the world has been
fundamentally altered by the nuclear arms race, by the rise of the
superpowers, by the explosive self-consciousness of the developing nations. Our assumption of American omnipotence has been shattered
by the most divisive and least successful war in our history; and, most
serious of all, our confidence and trust in our political, social, and
business institutions, and in each other, have been eroded in a
miasma of deception, intrigue, corruption, and, basically, subversion
of the very principles on which our political and social fabric depend.

Whether American democratic government as it is now organized is capable of handling those unprecedented issues in a satisfac-
tory manner is open to question; what hardly seems open to question
is the fact that in the process the functions of government itself have
become more distant from the citizen. In light of these changing conditions, it may be necessary to devise new forms, new guidelines, and
even new institutions to ensure that democratic government remains
democratic in the true sense.

The nation has only recently emerged from an experience that
emphasizes the point: the all but unperceived, easy slide toward authoritarianism and concentration of Executive power in the early
years of this decade, behind a democratic façade that deceived the
unwary into believing that all was well. In reality, if not in appearance, the government and the people had moved dangerously far
apart on many fronts by 1973—so far, in fact, that American democracy was headed for disaster from which it was saved in the first instance by an alert press and ultimately by the courts and Congress,
proving that even our most maligned institutions still have a formi-
dable inner strength.

The experience of Watergate demonstrates dramatically, in fact,
that as citizen and government have tended to become more distant
from each other, a free press has become more vital, more essential
than ever to the citizen, who perforce has to be more reliant upon it,
and upon the information it furnishes him, than he has ever been
before.

Yet the irony is that just as government, because of its size and
complexity, has distanced itself from the individual voter, so too the

press as an institution in our society seems to have distanced itself from the individual reader. Unfortunate as that development is—and it has profound implications for both the press and the country—it seems to me that it is an inevitable outgrowth of the kind of industrialized, mechanized, impersonalized civilization in which we are living. But it has to be corrected.

Willy-nilly, we have long since entered a world of big government, big business, big labor, big institutions—and big media. While the independent editor and the enterprising reporter and the critical commentator are still very much alive and flourishing, the fact remains that the intimate, almost personal relationship between newspaper and reader has tended to decline in direct proportion to the growth of newspapers as instruments of mass circulation and massive advertising, and their development as big business.

We are no longer in the era of the late eighteenth or early nineteenth centuries, when every person with an idea, political or otherwise, could become a printer and distribute a handbill, called a newspaper, expressing his views. We are no longer in the period when every large city in the country had half a dozen fiercely competing journals, ranging from one end of the political spectrum to the other. We are no longer in a time when it made no difference whether newspapers freely mixed news and editorial opinion, so long as they sold newspapers.

Today newspaper chains or groups control more than half the country's dailies and more than 60 per cent of total circulation. In less than 200 of the nation's 1500 cities which have daily newspapers is there more than one daily; and competing newspapers exist in only about 4 per cent of those 1500 cities—some 60 cities in all of the United States.

Newspaper chains have proliferated. That reflection of American business economics does not necessarily mean that the individual newspapers are less free than they were as individual entities; often, in fact, they are actually more free, because they are less dependent on local pressures than they otherwise might be. And, though it may seem strange, there are a number of striking cases of newspapers in so-called monopoly cities that are far superior, by every standard, to many newspapers in cities where there is competition. But there can be little doubt that the growth of newspaper chains, the elimination of competing newspapers, and the development of newspapers as big-business operations have helped to color adversely the public perception of the American press today.

It is not surprising that at this present turning point in our country's affairs, this Bicentennial, there should be new doubts about the role of the press, its relationship to government and the governed, its sense of responsibility, and its view of the future. As the power of the press has become more intensely concentrated as well as homogenized, so the burden of keeping the channels clear and clean becomes heavier, the conflicts of interest become sharper, the difficulty of searching out the truth and even of determining what the truth is becomes greater, and with it all the absolute necessity of protecting freedom—and of being able to justify that freedom—becomes more acute, perhaps more so than at any time in American history.

The American press in the world of today has taken on new dimensions—it is light years away from the easygoing political pamphleteering of the past. While the protection of the First Amendment remains the same as it was in 1791, the needs of the society that justified that special constitutional provision have grown infinitely more complex.

How can the public, as reliant on the press and other communications media as it is, come to a sensible conclusion on the great decisions it has to make in a working democracy, unless it has the maximum possible amount of information available to it—and information that is not controlled and spoon-fed to it by a government, no matter how benign and open that government may appear to be?

But the press has to do a great deal more than merely supply information. If it is to play its proper role in a viable democratic system, it cannot be a mere bulletin of yesterday's events. It has the obligation of searching out the movements and developments that affect our society—and our world—to interpret and analyze them, as well as to report them.

In that way, the press can serve as the medium through which the public can help shape events instead of perpetually being shaped by them. The American public is not to be relegated to the role of the public in most countries of the world, which is that of the passive recipient of events, that of the dumb beast. The American public has the intelligence—and the vigor—largely to determine for itself the out-come of events—if it has information and leadership, and if it has the basis to go on, a basis that only a free press can provide. And let us not forget that there are only a score of countries in the entire world where, by stretching a point or two, the press can be said to be free in any meaningful sense.

The American press thus has a leadership role: perhaps its high-est responsibility is to act as the conscience of the nation. The press—a free press—must speak out, or it runs the risk of becoming a mere bulletin board. It needs to speak out, not, of course, in one voice, but in a thousand voices. There is no monolithic or one-party press in our country, nor, so long as freedom exists, could there conceivably be one; and it is surely a basic obligation of a free press to offer lead-ership according to its own lights and its own conscience.

Considering the extraordinary technical developments that have been made in improving the speed and facility of communication, the record of the American press as a whole in carrying out its responsi-bility of informing and, even more important, in acting as the con-science of the American people, has been none too good. In most of the great crises of the postwar period, the press—at least in the initial stages—has been found wanting. It has tended to swallow the official viewpoint as though it were necessarily or even probably the truth. Along with the rest of the American people, the press, with few ex-ceptions, was panicked by McCarthy in the 1950's; blinded by Viet-nam in the 1960's; deceived by the White House in the 1970's.

But the press has gradually learned from its initial failure in each of those cases; it knows that it has the inescapable obligation to illuminate the reality behind the appearance. The ultimate triumph of Watergate proved the point; and if following that course now tends to place the press in an adversary position *vis-à-vis* not only gov-ernment but any or all other institutions, so much the better for us and for them, and, most of all, for the public.

The adversary position is indeed the natural position for a press that takes seriously its obligation to uncover what is wrong, or venal, or corrupt in public life, or with private institutions or individuals whose activities affect the public interest.

In fact, the American press is only now beginning—for the first time in at least a half-century—to examine in depth the questionable role of corporate business in public affairs, whether the question raised be bribery to obtain defense contracts abroad or bribery to obtain political favors at home. I think that as time goes on, our press will be devoting increasing attention to that aspect of its investigatory role as public watchdog.

But there is another and much more difficult problem, which is the obverse of that one. It is the one we have heard most about in recent months, and will hear a great deal more about in the future. The question is raised with growing intensity whether the press does not often have the responsibility of making the judgment *not* to publish—the responsibility of self-restraint, of withholding a potentially dangerous secret, of refusing to publish details that could damage a nation's security or an individual's reputation.

That is the other side of press responsibility, and it presents a problem of conscience and of ethics which has not been satisfactorily resolved from Washington's day to this.

In wartime, it is relatively easy. I believe the Chicago *Tribune*, for example, was guilty of criminal irresponsibility when it revealed at the height of World War II that the United States had broken the Japanese code, or when the *Tribune* and the late, unlamented Washington *Times-Herald* revealed detailed military plans of the United States—three days, as it happened, before Pearl Harbor.

But the real problem is in peacetime, especially in this era, when it is virtually impossible, at least in our free and open society—whether in the sprawling bureaucracy, the Congress, the White House, or even the grand jury room—to keep a secret from the prying eyes of the press. And the real question for the responsible newspaper is: whether it should keep that secret, or should reveal it, and if so, when? Certainly the mere classification of a document is not signal enough. I doubt that it would be seriously argued today that publication of the Pentagon papers involved any damage to the nation whatsoever, or did anything but throw some useful light on the inner history of the Vietnam War. It is unfortunate but true that official classification has been too often misused by American bureaucracy, civilian and military, for it any longer to be taken as an absolute barrier to publication, automatically outweighing all other considerations.

Yet when the President of the United States requested a newspaper, in the national interest, to refrain from publishing news of an impending action—the Bay of Pigs invasion is a classic example— was it responsible or irresponsible for the newspaper to defer to the President's wishes? I think, in the context of the time, the failure to publish was in that case entirely responsible; but others strongly differ, on the grounds that it was unwarranted interference with freedom of the press and that the nation would have been far better off if it had been forewarned of that illegal act of war taking place with official sanction.

Recently, the newspapers have had to decide whether to publish secret information about past intelligence activities of both the F.B.I. and the C.I.A. When such reports come into a newspaper's possession, is it responsible—or reprehensible—to publish them? Who is to say?

The dilemma is a terribly real one. I know of no newspaperman who wants to damage the national security; yet I know of no newspaperman who is not extremely skeptical, and with cause, of the phrase "national security" when used as a wrapper—as it has so often been in the past—to clothe matters that the public has a right to know. The press must be constantly on the alert against the potential misuse of the "national security" label to cover error, venality, corruption, or, most ominously, a drift toward authoritarianism and personal rule.

However, each time information allegedly having to do with national security is published in the American press, the question is unavoidable: are we taking undue advantage of our First Amendment privilege to the detriment of the nation, or are we acting in the public interest? Previous newspaper disclosures of hitherto secret activities of the intelligence agencies have surely turned out to be a public service, and have already led to proposals for major reforms designed to keep those agencies from ever again becoming a threat to the democratic process. Each case must be decided on its merits, but each legitimately raises anew the question of press freedom versus press responsibility. However, the public has to realize that that responsibility often involves the questioning of institutions, making establishments uncomfortable, and opening up new areas of concern and discussion.

Freedom and responsibility are not only not incompatible so far as the American press is concerned; they are reciprocal, and, in fact, indispensable to each other. For once the public becomes convinced—however wrongly—that the press does not deserve that guarantee which the Founding Fathers felt was essential to free government, the legal protection will be hollow, as Hamilton forewarned, and the freedom will become a sham.

Already, in fact, the freedom of the press in the United States is under serious attack, an attack more far-reaching and pernicious than most people realize and surely more pervasive than at any time since the Sedition Act of nearly two centuries ago. It takes various forms, emanating from all three branches of government—perhaps as a tangential spin-off from Watergate; perhaps as a reflection of the demonstrable loss of public confidence in all institutions, including the press; perhaps from genuine concern that the press is misinterpreting its First Amendment liberty as unlimited license.

In any case, as the press has assumed the responsibility in recent years of inquiring into and exposing what had been the hidden recesses of government—Executive, Legislative, and Judicial—the reaction on the part of governing authority has been to attempt to place new and unaccustomed restrictions on America's free press. The federal government's effort to impose prior censorship on national security grounds in peacetime, the first such attempt in modern history, in the Pentagon Papers Case, was struck down by the Supreme Court. However, other and relatively new kinds of restrictions are now being placed on the press with growing frequency. The "gag order" is one—a form of prior censorship increasingly used in lower federal and state courts, usually forbidding the press to publish certain material on the ground that to do so would endanger the defendant's right to fair trial. That question is in fact at issue before the Supreme Court of the United States at the very moment of this writing, and on its resolution may depend the freedom of the American press from potential or incipient judicial tyranny.

The First Amendment guarantee of free press and the Sixth Amendment guarantee of fair trial may on occasion come into conflict; the question is a real one and is under constant scrutiny and discussion by both press and courts. But the loose employment of the gag order carries with it such dangerous implications of censorship and could so easily prevent the exposure of corruption or error—or both—in the judicial process, that in fighting these orders the press is in fact defending the public's cause as much as its own.

Similarly, the repeated use of the subpoena power in recent years to force newspapermen to testify before grand juries or to reveal their sources in criminal cases represents another potentially crippling attack on press and public freedom, for the very basic reason that confidentiality of sources lies at the very heart of the newspaper's ability to investigate wrongdoing on the part of both government officials and private individuals.

Pending legislation in Congress carries still further the threat to press freedom in America of the 1970's. A major revision of the federal criminal code, Senate Bill #1, contains several proposed sections sweepingly extending both the concept of national security information and the government's power to conceal, under that cover, just the kind of evidence of wrongdoing that has been exposed by a vigilant press in recent years. Had such legislation been in effect, the threat to democratic institutions represented by secret, illegal, and virtually uncontrolled actions of the nation's primary intelligence agencies, as well as other executive agencies of government, would probably never have been known, and surely it would not have been caught in time.

The press has a special duty in our constitutional democracy, imposed on it from the beginning, to serve as protector of the public interest against untoward accretions of power by one or all of the three branches of government. In a peculiarly American sense, the press is indeed Burke's "Fourth Estate," and must remain independently so. But the government also has a responsibility of protecting its own confidentiality. It can best do so not by imposing restrictions on the press, which would almost surely undercut the First Amendment, but by tightening its internal controls—in the same way that the courts would surely do better to impose sanctions on officers of the court to forestall leaks rather than introduce censorship, with its pernicious implications.

But the problem remains. The press does not help its case by insisting on an absolutist position, by regarding the First Amendment as automatically overriding every other provision of the Constitution, not to mention common sense. The press has the obligation, a public obligation, to fight every Executive, Judicial or Legislative attempt to erode its liberty, but at the same time it is not going to retain—or regain—public confidence if it is constantly perceived to be arrogant, unwilling to recognize conflicting rights, or not too concerned about maintaining the most rigid standards to protect and preserve its own integrity.

For example, the *adversary* relationship toward government, desirable and healthy as it is, must not be allowed within the news columns to turn into an *advocacy* role. It has become fashionable in recent years to scoff at the ideal of objective news reporting, and it is true that total objectivity in newspapers is almost a contradiction in terms. Human beings report, write, and edit the news; and human beings are subjective, inevitably putting themselves into the story that comes out in tonight's or tomorrow's paper.

But the crucial question is: how much of themselves, their opinions, passions, judgments? To the degree that personalization, or advocacy journalism, is encouraged and permitted in the news columns of the daily newspaper and disguised as reporting, to that degree the basic responsibility of the paper to the public is dishonored, and credibility, its most precious asset, is destroyed.

It is, of course, difficult to prove that the relative lack of public confidence in the press is very much greater today than it was twenty or fifty or even a hundred years ago; but it is not difficult to prove that it is much more dangerous today than it ever was—more dangerous for the press itself and therefore more dangerous for the preservation of American freedom.

As confidence in all institutions has been weakened; as our society has at the same time grown more complex, more broadly sophisticated, and less trustful; and as newspaper management has tended to move steadily away from the personally directed journalism of an individual editor and toward the impersonality of the corporate structure, the newspaper's direct relationship to the public has inevitably become more distant, and the public understanding of the inextricable interconnection between press liberty and public liberty has become blurred. The extraordinary growth in attacks on press freedom in recent years is at one and the same time a reflection of public disillusionment with all systems, including ours, and a specific indication that freedom of the press under the First Amendment is constantly endangered and has constantly to be fought for.

A great deal has been heard in recent years—and properly so—about the right of newspapers' access to the records, documents, and files of government. The Freedom of Information Act, imperfect though it is, has somewhat improved matters. But although we newspapermen are generally highly articulate about the public's right of access to government, as we should be, we are not usually quite so vocal about the public's right of access to ourselves.

Governmentally enforced access to the press is not the answer. Far from it. To force a newspaper to publish an item is no less an infringement on its freedom than to forbid it from publishing one. Nevertheless, the public demand for greater accessibility to the press is not to be laughed off—and I believe that in one form or another the threat of governmentally enforced access will lurk in the dark corners of the public mind just as long as there is a public perception, however wrong it may be, that newspapers tend to operate less in the public interest than in their own.

Newspapers, in fact, have to be accountable to something more than their own business offices and stockholders; they have to be accountable first of all to their own consciences, of course, but in the broadest sense they must be accountable to the public interest as well.

Since any governmental enforcement of accessibility in news or editorial columns must by its very nature involve unacceptable—and illegal—interference in violation of the First Amendment, it seems to me that we newspapermen have a special obligation to retain or regain public confidence, through conscious and deliberate effort to open ourselves to the public, and to pay particular attention to complaints of unfairness, inaccuracy, bias, and vindictiveness—that is, to make ourselves *voluntarily* accountable. Some newspapers have already gone a considerable distance in doing just that, but not many, and certainly not enough. Establishment of the News Council, an independent, disinterested body with no power but moral force, is one way of providing a public channel of complaint; but it is not the only way; there are many others, such as the use of an "ombudsman" on individual newspapers.

However, if there comes to be a widespread public conviction that the press is a closed institution and therefore not to be trusted, or that the press is willing to defy the national interest or trample on individual rights in order to sell papers, the threat of serious restrictions on press freedom will become very real—and the result, as a college president recently said, will be "far more damaging to the national interest than any [restrictions] resulting from a responsible self-restraint by the press."

In this era every value is being reexamined and every right is under question, even the constitutional protection of freedom of the press. In my view it has to be defended from the kind of attack to which it is even now being subjected, not only for the good of the press but, much more importantly, for the good of the public. The legal right inherent in the First Amendment carries with it a moral obligation, a kind of moral compact between press and people. That is not something which can be enforced; but it is something that the press will ignore at its own and the country's peril.

The American press requires the freedom to carry out its responsibilities now more than ever before—as the institutions of government, business, and society must change to meet the challenges of this technologically revolutionary age, and do so within the democratic framework. But we of the press will only succeed in preserving that freedom so long as we are willing to fight for it—and equally important, so long as the American public remains convinced, as in the past, that we deserve it.